Contemporary Wire Wrapped Jewelry

Curtis Kenneth Leonard with William A. Kappele

Gem Guides Book Co.

315 Cloverleaf Drive, Suite F • Baldwin Park, CA 91706

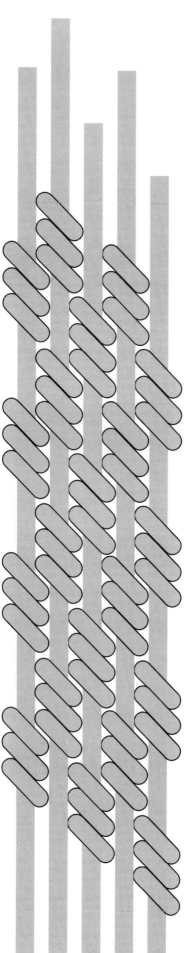

Copyright ©1995
GEM GUIDES BOOK CO.

First Edition 1995

Printed and bound in the United States of America.

ISBN: 0-935182-71-3

Library of Congress Catalog No. 95-75187

CONTENTS

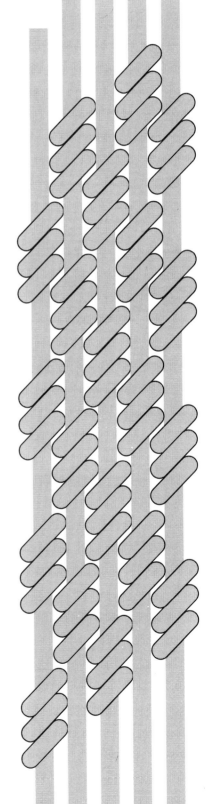

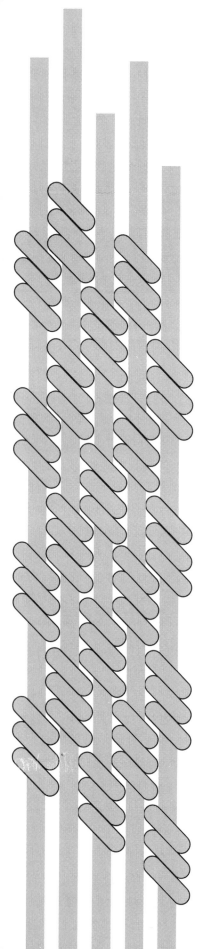

Introduction

Welcome to Wire Wrapping

Although there are many methods used in the art of jewelry making, none offer the advantages of wire wrapping. Silversmithing and gold-smithing require a fairly impressive and expensive set of tools; and lost wax casting requires not only the metalsmith's tools, but also an expensive and often bulky casting machine, a torch, and a burnout oven, in addition to a large workshop space. By contrast, the art of wire wrapping is successfully practiced with a bare minimum of tools, materials, and space. All the tools and materials needed to create beautiful jewelry can be carried in a shoe-box, and the workspace requirements are no larger than a spot in the kitchen or even on a coffee table.

For those whose workspace is shared with other activities, wire wrapping offers another advantage—virtually no mess. Unlike other jewelry crafts, there is no pickle pot, no torch, no solder, and no buffing and polishing machines to create dust. Those who use a motor tool for polishing can easily hold the tool and the work inside a box to limit the amount of dust generated.

Finally, the cost conscious will really appreciate wire wrapping. The tools are few, inexpensive, and very basic, and the wire, even gold-filled, is not at all prohibitive. Cut and polished stones and cabochons are readily available for anywhere from a few cents to a few dollars. However, wire wrapped jewelry should not be ranked with inexpensive craft techniques that merely require gluing stones to a purchased finding. The quality and value of the finished product can easily rival those produced by the far more technical and expensive methods and, like them, is a genuine article of jewelry.

About This Book

In this book, Curtis Kenneth Leonard will take you step by step through the basic techniques of wire wrapping. Through the use of clear, concise text, detailed photographs, and full size pattern drawings, you will be able to master the skills of wire wrapping and, by the time you finish your last project, you will be prepared to design and produce unique jewelry pieces that will be the envy of all who see them.

There are a number of books on the market that attempt to teach the craft of wire wrapping. Most use photographs *or* line drawings to illustrate the techniques described in the text. Realizing that some people learn best with photographs and others with line drawings, when developing this book, we chose to use both. While other books use photographs that are often cluttered with views of hands, knuckles, and tools that obscure the view of the piece, this book uses photographs that were taken on a lightbox, completely eliminating shadows and confusing backgrounds. Only the applicable piece and a tool, if absolutely necessary, are included.

Although the projects are not necessarily arranged in sequential order, we recommend that beginning wrappers begin with project 1, since the accompanying photographs include arrows pointing to the appropriate operation discussed in the text. First-timers may be more comfortable practicing with some inexpensive wire until they get the feel of the process; beyond that, however, the wrapper should feel free to work with any of the projects.

A special section between projects 11 and 12 will help the prospective wire wrapper design his or her own projects. Project 12 consists of two pendants developed with the techniques used in this section.

How to Use the Patterns

One of the unique features of this book is the use of patterns for each step in a piece's construction. When necessary, dimensions are given on these patterns. They are most useful in determining how well the wrap is conforming to the basic shape of the piece. Simply lay the project on the pattern to verify the shape of the piece and the position of the wraps. The wraps are indicated by boxes; any wrap that falls inside the box is within tolerance and is just fine. We think the reader will find these patterns greatly beneficial, and will result in far less reworking.

Tools And Materials

One of the beauties of wire wrapping is that very few tools are needed, and these are usually found in the toolbox of anyone who dabbles in jewelry making or general crafts. The following list includes everything you will need for beginning to advanced work. As you gain experience, you may want to make some special tools to simplify such tasks as scrolling.

Cutters

The diagonal (left) and end cutting (right) pliers are the wire wrapper's basic cutting tools. Both work well—just choose the one that feels best to you.

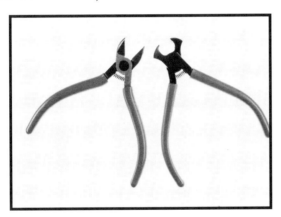

Flat Nose Pliers

The flat nose pliers are used to hold wire for twisting, to hold the hook while bending the wraps, and to crimp the wrap when finished.

Round Nose and Chain Nose Pliers

The round nose (right) and chain nose (left) are used primarily for scrolling. The type you use is largely a matter of feel. If you choose the chain nose, be certain to get the type with smooth jaws. Many chain nose pliers have a toothed pattern on the inside of the jaws that provide a better grip, but will badly damage your wire.

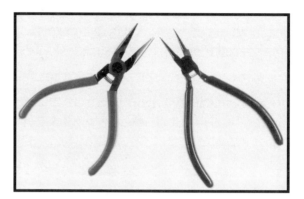

Swiss Files

A small set of Swiss pattern files is essential for removing sharp edges from the cut wire ends and for doing minor shaping and smoothing.

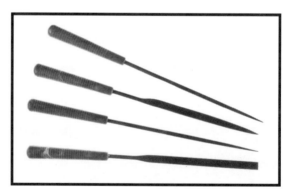

Pin Vise

A pin vise is absolutely necessary for twisting decorative wires. Pin vises are available in several styles, but the most practical is the double-ended type with reversible collets such as the one shown here. They cost a little more than the single collet type, but provide the ability to handle four different wire sizes by utilizing removable and reversible jaw inserts.

Scale

Although this book provides full size patterns that eliminate the need for measurements, you should have a small scale and learn to use it if you plan to do much wire wrapping.

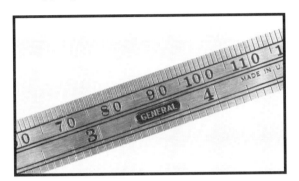

Finally, you will need a jeweler's polishing cloth to remove oxidation and put a protective shine on your projects, and a pen or soft pencil for marking wrap placements.

A few of the optional tools you might want to purchase include:

A ring mandrel to aid in bending the wire bundle to shape.

A ring sizer to help in getting ring shanks just right.

A motor tool (such as the Dremel) and polishing discs for polishing.

Basic Techniques

Wire wrapping techniques are uncomplicated and easily mastered. If you study the pictures and descriptions carefully and practice each step a few times with some scrap or inexpensive wire, you will be ready to tackle your first project with confidence.

Cutting

Cutting really needs very little discussion as a technique. It is necessary to use sharp cutters, and to cut squarely across the wire as close to your line as possible in order to limit the amount of filing.

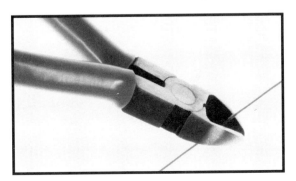

Materials

Jewelry wire is available in a wide variety of gauges and shapes. Gauge is the term used for the thickness of the wire. The standard American Wire Gauge is the Brown and Sharpe (B&S). This is usually listed as ASG (American Standard Gauge), or AWG (American Wire Gauge). Your supplier will help you with the terms. It is important to remember that the higher the number, the finer the wire. For example, an 8-gauge wire is considerably thicker than a 24-gauge wire.

The standard shapes available are:
Round
Square
Half Round
Double Half Round
Triangular
Flat
Patterned (Floral, Engraved, Brite Cut, etc.)

The standard metal types are :
Brass
Copper
Fine Silver
Sterling Silver
1/20 Gold-filled
14 KT Gold.

Typical wire gauge sizes for wire wrapping are: 8, 12, 16, 18, 20, 22, 24, and 26

Temporary Binding Wire

Using the temporary binding wire correctly is one of the more important steps in wire wrap jewelry making. The wire is cleaner and easier to work with than tape, which is frequently used. Use regular beading wire and wrap it just tight enough to keep your bundle of wires from slipping out of position.

Twisting

Twisting is the most basic decorative technique. The wire is held at one end by the pin vise and at the opposite end by the flat nose pliers. In some cases, you will be required to twist until the end in the pin vise breaks off, and other times you will twist *gently* until you get the effect you wish. In the latter case, particularly if you are twisting more than one wire, *go slowly,* taking only small turns. It is wise to count the turns so that the twist patterns will match. Keep notes so that you can recreate the look on later projects.

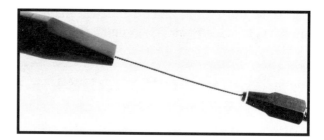

Wrapping

Wrapping is the technique that gives this style of jewelry making its name. It is done by forming a hook on the end of a wire, placing the hook over the wire bundle, and wrapping tightly for the required number of turns while holding the hook on the wire bundle with the flat nose pliers. The wraps should be kept close together during the process to avoid a lot of adjusting. When the required number of wraps have been made, the wire is cut off as close to the bundle as possible.

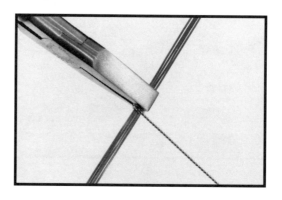

Crimping

Crimping is the process of flattening and tightening the wraps. It is done with the flat nose pliers and must be done firmly enough to secure the wrap, but not so firmly that the metal is damaged. With a little practice, you will develop just the right touch.

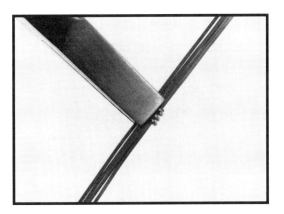

Filing

Filing is done with the Swiss pattern files on the cut ends of the wire. You must be very careful not to nick or otherwise damage the surface of the wires by overzealous filing. It is only necessary to remove sharp edges so that they will not snag on skin or clothing.

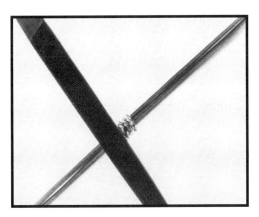

Scrolling

Scrolling is the process of rolling the ends of the wire into small loops for decoration and to find a place for the ends of the wire bundles. Scrolling is done with the round nose or chain nose pliers. Grip the metal at the cut end and gently roll around the nose of the pliers. It is important to keep the scrolls on opposite pieces of the work uniform. This will be made easier for you if you mark various size positions on your pliers with one of the files.

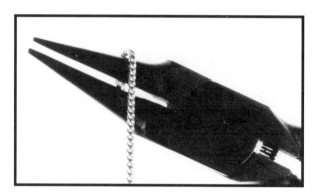

Shaping

Shaping is the means of bending the wire bundle to the shape of the stone in your piece. One means is to use the stone itself or one of similar size as a form for the bending. Another method is to use a ring mandrel to shape the rounds or ellipses. Work slowly and carefully to avoid kinking the wire bundle.

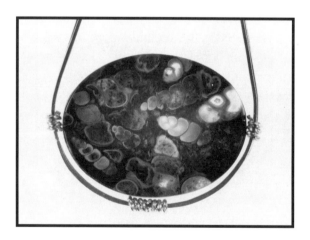

Tips For Wire Wrappers

1. When cutting wire, it is very important to wear safety goggles to keep tiny snippets from flying into your eyes.

2. Always file the cut ends of wires to remove sharp burrs that can scratch the skin or snag clothing.

3. The wire used in this book is typically 20-gauge. This is thicker than that used by most wire wrappers, but the thicker wire provides the piece with a much stronger base and greatly decreases the possibility of the piece being crushed or deformed.

4. Many wire wrappers use masking tape to temporarily bind the wire bundles, but this method leaves a residue that can be a nuisance to remove. It is much neater to use a 22 or 24-gauge beading wire.

5. The choice of a stone for a project is, of course, a personal one, but it is important to make sure that the colors of the stone and the metal complement each other. All stones look fine in gold and, although turquoise and silver is a classic combination, some stones such as jade, fire agate, and yellow or orange stones tend to clash with silver wire.

6. The only polishing a wire wrapped project really needs can be done with a polishing cloth. Rouge cloths work great! They cut through the tarnish and impart a barrier to slow down the tarnishing process. If you are in a real hurry, a one-inch cotton or muslin buff charged with rouge and used on a motor tool will work very well. Only polish the wire bundle while it is flat, and make sure to hold or clamp the bundle securely.

7. If you plan to use soft stones such as opal, turquoise, or rhodocrosite, it is advisable to form wire bends to calibrated sizes around a ring mandrel or a same-size quartz stone to avoid chipping the soft stone. It is also a good idea to make the cage loose enough so that the stone "floats" in the mounting without touching the border. For an uncalibrated stone, push the stone into some floral clay to make a mold. Fill the mold with epoxy and allow it to harden. This gives you a model to form your bends around. Once the bends are completed, finish the project as usual.

8. Save your clippings. They can be used to add texture if you decide to take up silver or goldsmithing. If you do enough wire wrapping, you may accumulate enough metal to use in lost wax casting. You could even melt it down and redraw it to make more wire. If none of this appeals to you, you can always sell your scraps to a precious metals dealer.

Now that we have covered the basics, let's begin!

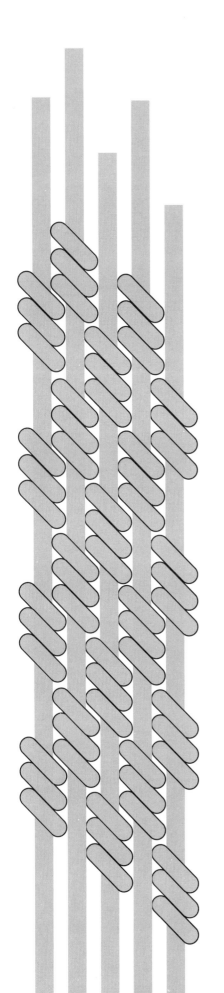

P R O J E C T 1

Filigree Wire Cage Pin

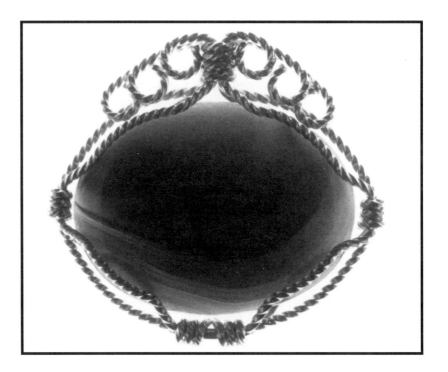

This project is a wonderful introduction to wire wrapping techniques. Mastering the steps shown here will help you on your way to making everything your imagination can create.

① Measure and cut four 6-inch pieces of wire.

② Bind three of the wires together into a flat bundle and secure each end with temporary binding wire. Measure and mark the center point of the bundle (see fig. 1).

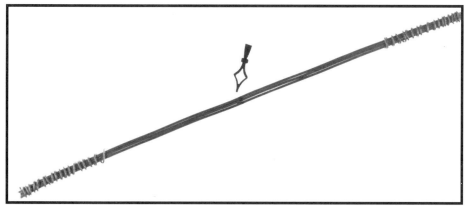

FIG. 1

③ Check your bundle against pattern 1.

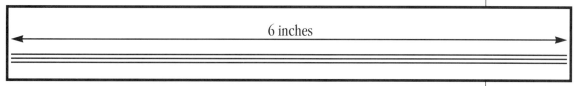

6 inches

PATTERN 1

TOOLS REQUIRED:
Pin vise
Pliers
Swiss file set
Polishing cloth

OPTIONAL TOOLS:
Ring mandrel

MATERIALS REQUIRED:
24 inches of
  20-gauge square
  wire
One 30x22mm
  cabochon
One 3/4-inch
  pin back
Temporary binding
  wire
5-minute epoxy glue

4 Secure one end of the remaining fourth wire in the pin vise and hold the opposite end with the flat nose pliers. Twist the wire clockwise until the end in the pin vise breaks off. This twisted wire will supply the material for the wraps (see fig. 2).

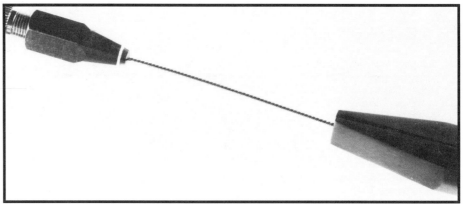

FIG. 2

5 Form a hook on one end of your twisted wire using flat nose pliers (see fig. 3).

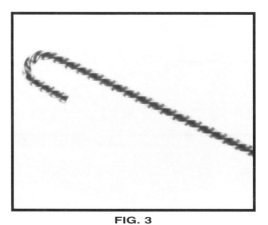

FIG. 3

Check the size and curve of your twisted wire hook against pattern 2.

Wrap wire side view

Wrap wire top view (right wrap)

Wrap wire top view (left wrap)

PATTERN 2

Place the hook of your twisted wire over the three-wire bundle just to the right of the center mark with the long end of the twisted wire on top of the bundle and hold it with the flat nose pliers. Wrap the wire three turns to the right. Cut off the twisted wire with the last (third) wrap on the bottom of the bundle. Form another hook and repeat the operation on the left side of the bundle's center mark. Be sure to wrap to the left (see figs. 4&5). Crimp the wraps with the flat nose pliers.

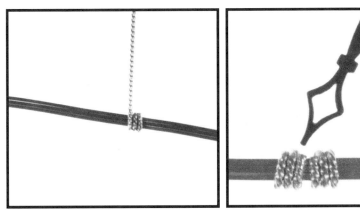

FIG. 4 (LEFT) AND FIG. 5 (RIGHT)

8 Check your wrap positions against pattern 3. Be certain your cutoffs are on the bottom of the bundle.

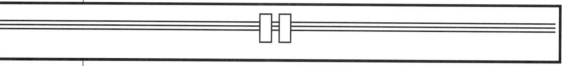

PATTERN 3

9 Remove the temporary binding wire and lay the bundle flat on your work surface. Fan out the two top wires on each side. Hold the right wrap with your flat nose pliers and, with the pin vise, twist the two right-hand wires clockwise and the two left-hand wires counter-clockwise (see fig. 6).

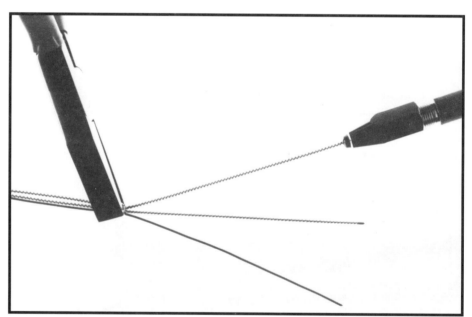

FIG. 6

10 Check your work against pattern 4.

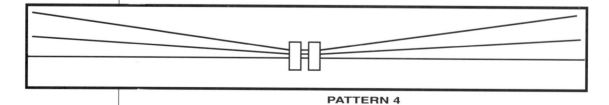

PATTERN 4

11 If your piece matches the full size pattern, reform the bundle and rewrap the ends with the temporary binding wire. Refer to pattern 5 and mark the positions of the next wraps. Form another hook in your piece of twisted wire, place it on the right side of the bundle at your mark and wrap it as you did for the center wraps. Cut the wire, bend another hook, and repeat the process on the left side. Remember to wrap the right wire to the right and the left wire to the left (see fig. 7). Crimp the wraps with the flat nose pliers.

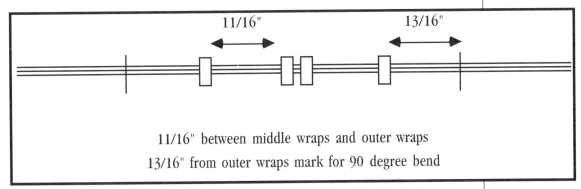

11/16"   13/16"

11/16" between middle wraps and outer wraps
13/16" from outer wraps mark for 90 degree bend

PATTERN 5

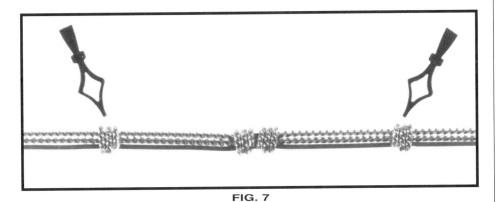

FIG. 7

12 At this point you should file all of the cut ends on your wrap wires with a flat Swiss file. Be sure that all sharp spots are removed, taking care not to nick or damage the other wires. When all sharp spots have been eliminated, polish the whole project carefully with your polishing cloth.

13 Now, using either your cabochon or your ring mandrel at size 10, begin to form the shape of the outer cage. Begin by placing the middle point of the long side of the ellipse of the cabochon next to the middle wraps of your bundle. Slowly bend the bundle so that it conforms to the shape of the cabochon. Continue to work around the small ends of the cabochon and onto the top. Let the ends of the bundle cross at the top. Mark the top center point and carefully bend the ends of the bundle up at almost a 90-degree angle. The ends of the bundle should now be pointing upward from the stone, and the bundle should conform to its shape. Make any necessary adjustments so that the fit is precise, but be careful not to bend anything too far or to kink the wires. Bind the ends of the bundle together as shown in fig. 8 and check your work against pattern 6.

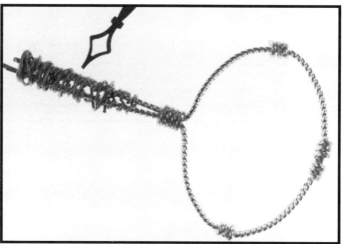

FIG. 8 (ABOVE) AND PATTERN 6 (BELOW)

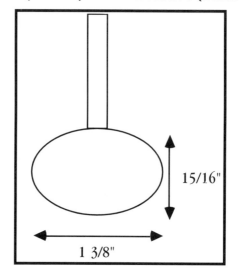

15/16"

1 3/8"

14 Form another hook on your twisted wire and place it as close to the bends in the bundle as possible (see fig. 9). Holding the hook against the bundle with the flat nose pliers, wrap four turns upward toward the bundle ends. Crimp the wrap with the flat nose pliers.

FIG. 9

15 To form the stone prongs on the back of the pin, grip the square un-twisted wire with the flat nose pliers at a point halfway between the wraps and pull it gently toward the center of the cage (see fig. 10). Repeat the process for the remaining three prongs. Be careful to grip the prongs at the same spot and pull them the same distance to keep the pin symmetrical.

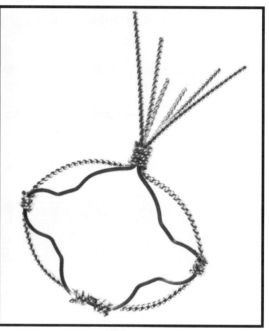

FIG. 10

16 Check your work against pattern 7

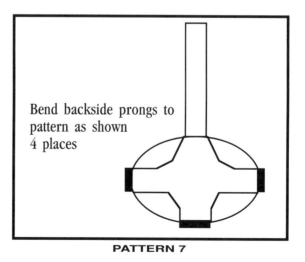

Bend backside prongs to pattern as shown 4 places

PATTERN 7

17 Remove the temporary binding wire at the top of the bundles. With the pin vise, twist the remaining two square wires. Twist the right-hand wire clockwise and the left-hand wire counterclockwise.

18 Check pattern 8 for the correct length of the top wires and cut them accordingly. File the cut ends with the Swiss file to remove any sharp spots. Place the stone in the cage and close the cage by forming the front prongs. To form the prongs, grip the twisted wire at a spot just next to the wrap and bend upward gently. Repeat the operation at the other wrap, then carefully bend a curve in the middle to match the curve of the cabochon. Do this with the remaining three prongs. Press each prong to make sure that it is snug against the stone (see fig. 11).

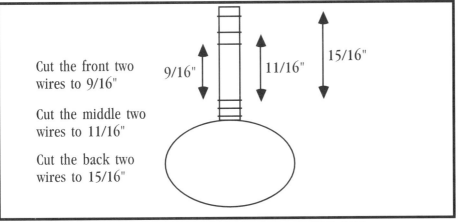

Cut the front two wires to 9/16"

Cut the middle two wires to 11/16"

Cut the back two wires to 15/16"

9/16"   11/16"   15/16"

PATTERN 8 (ABOVE) AND FIG. 11 (BELOW)

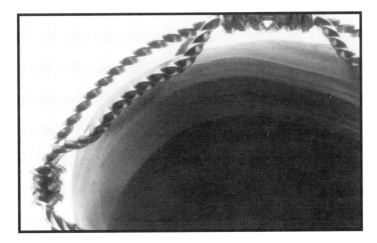

19 With the round nose or chain nose pliers, grip a twisted wire closest to the center and carefully roll it into the position shown in Fig. 12. Continue the same procedure working outward from the center.

FIG. 12

20 Check the prongs to be sure they are symmetrical, and make any fine adjustments to the shape of the pin or position of wires. Give the pin a final polishing with a jeweler's cloth.

21 Rough up the back of the cabochon with emery paper and bond the pin back to your project with 5-minute epoxy cement (see fig. 13) and allow to dry thoroughly. Congratulations! You have completed your first project!

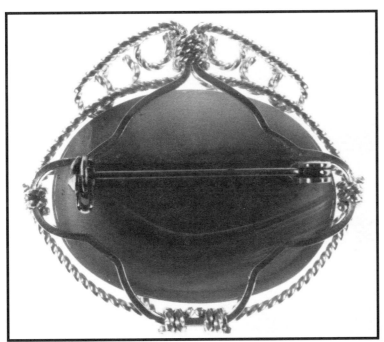

FIG. 13

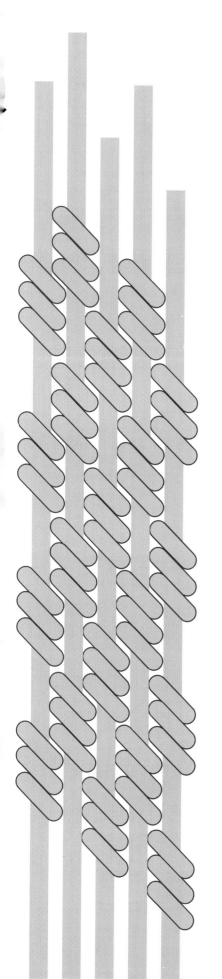

P R O J E C T 2

Pearl Drop Earrings

1 Cut seven 5-inch pieces of the 20-gauge wire.

2 Bind three of the wires together at each end with the temporary binding wire. Mark the center point of the bundle (see fig. 1). Repeat the process with three more wires to make the other earring.

FIG. 1

3 Check your work against pattern 1.

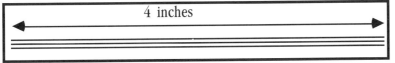

4 inches

PATTERN 1

4 Place one end of the remaining wire into the pin vise, hold the other end with the flat nose pliers, and twist the wire clockwise until the end in the pin vise breaks off (see fig. 2).

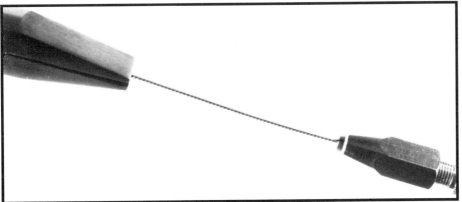

FIG. 2

TOOLS REQUIRED:
Pin vise
Pliers
Swiss file set
Polishing cloth

MATERIALS REQUIRED:
35 inches of 20-gauge square wire
Two 10mm gem balls or imitation pearls, (undrilled)
One pair of fishhook style earwires or ball dangle earstuds
Temporary Binding Wire

5 With the flat nose pliers, form one end of the twisted wire into a hook (see fig. 3).

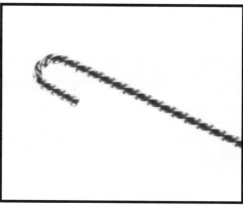

FIG. 3

6 Check your work against pattern 2.

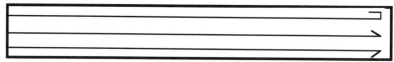

PATTERN 2

7 Place the hook end of your twisted wire over the bundle with the short end on the bottom. Align the long end of the twisted wire with the right side of your center mark. Hold the twisted wire with the flat nose pliers and wrap two turns to your right. Cut off the twisted wire at the edge of the bundle (see fig. 4). Bend another hook and repeat the process for the other earring.

FIG. 4

8 Check your work against pattern 3.

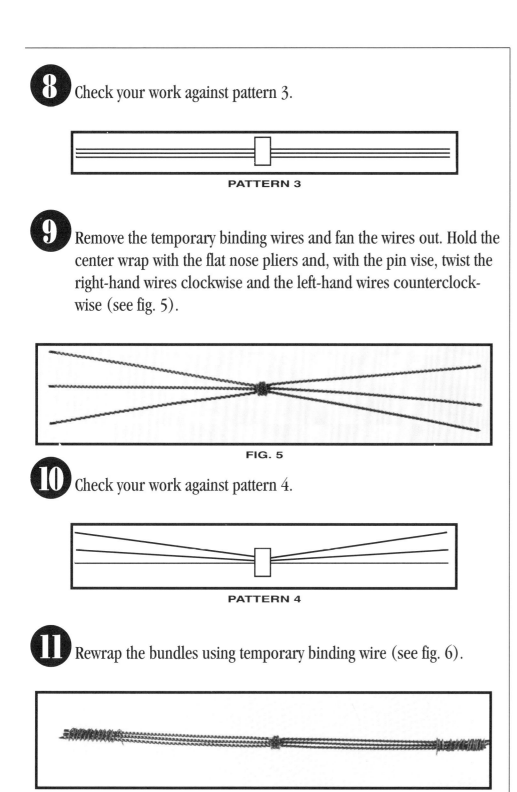

PATTERN 3

9 Remove the temporary binding wires and fan the wires out. Hold the center wrap with the flat nose pliers and, with the pin vise, twist the right-hand wires clockwise and the left-hand wires counterclockwise (see fig. 5).

FIG. 5

10 Check your work against pattern 4.

PATTERN 4

11 Rewrap the bundles using temporary binding wire (see fig. 6).

FIG. 6

12 File the cut ends of the wraps with a Swiss file. Be sure that all sharp spots are eliminated. Polish the bundles with your jeweler's cloth.

13 Form the bundles to the shape of your gem balls. It is possible to use the gem balls themselves as the forming mold, but they are hard to hold steady while bending the bundles. It is probably better to find a piece of dowel rod, a felt pen barrel, or some other item of similar size and shape from around the house to use as a forming tool. When you find just the right one, keep it in your tool kit for future projects (see fig. 7).

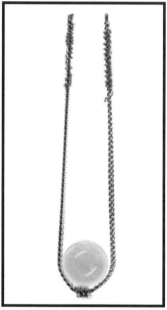

FIG. 7

14 Lace the bundle ends together with the temporary binding wire (see fig. 8A) and check your work against pattern 5.

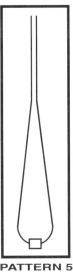

PATTERN 5

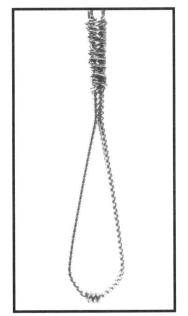
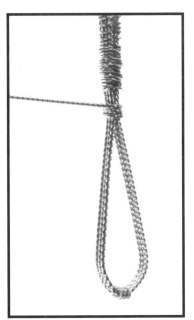

FIG. 8A (LEFT) AND FIG. 8B (RIGHT)

15 Form a hook in your twisted wire and place it 1 1/2 inches from the bend. Hold the hook to the bundle with the flat nose pliers and wrap three turns toward the bundle ends (see fig. 8B). Form another hook in your twisted wire and repeat the process on the other earring.

Note

Be extremely careful with a knife blade. If your scale is not thin enough, you might want to use a table knife.

16 Check your work against pattern 6.

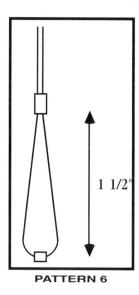

1 1/2"

PATTERN 6

17 Form the cage for the gem balls by inserting the edge of your steel scale or a knife blade between the wires and bending them outward (see fig. 9).

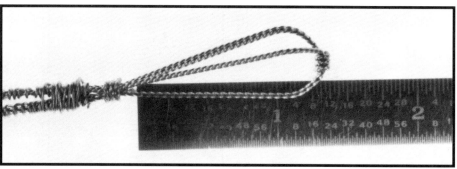

FIG. 9

18 Remove the temporary binding wire from the top of each bundle and fan the wires out to prepare them for cutting.

19 Cut the wires at the top of the earrings to the lengths shown on pattern 7. File the cut ends with a Swiss file. Be certain that you completely remove all sharp spots.

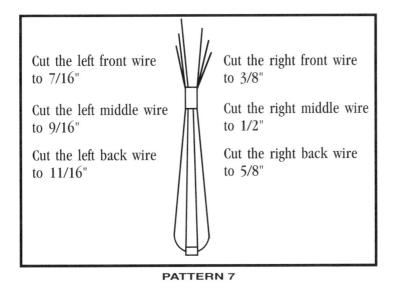

Cut the left front wire to 7/16"

Cut the right front wire to 3/8"

Cut the left middle wire to 9/16"

Cut the right middle wire to 1/2"

Cut the left back wire to 11/16"

Cut the right back wire to 5/8"

PATTERN 7

20 Press the gem balls into the cages and carefully bend the wires to close the cages (see fig. 10).

FIG. 10

21 With the round nose pliers, carefully bend the scrolls. Begin at the front of the cage and work toward the back (see fig. 11). Give the earrings a final polishing with the jeweler's cloth.

FIG. 11

22 Attach the earwires or the ball dangle studs to the highest loop on the earrings (see fig. 12). You now have a beautiful pair of earrings.

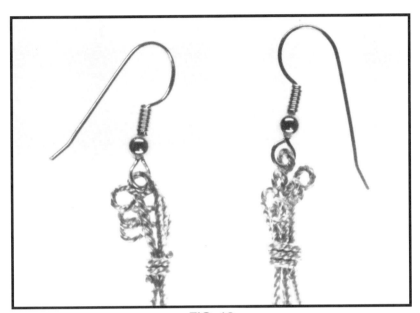

FIG. 12

P R O J E C T **3**

Bar Dangle Charm Pin

This project gives you the flexibility of creating a unique piece of jewelry with the addition of your own charm or a wire-wrapped stone.

1 Cut five 3-inch pieces and one 6-inch piece of square wire.

2 Lay out the five 3-inch wires making certain that they are as flat and straight as possible. Bind each end with temporary binding wire (see fig. 1).

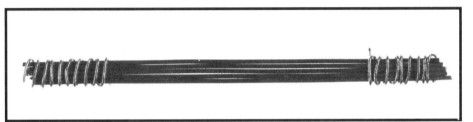

FIG. 1

3 Measure and mark the center point of the bundle and check your work against pattern 1.

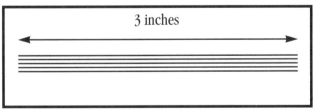

3 inches

PATTERN 1

4 Check one more time that your wires are flat and straight. Correct any problems by carefully bending and twisting.

TOOLS REQUIRED:
Pin vise
Pliers
Swiss file set
Polishing cloth

MATERIALS REQUIRED:
21 inches of 20-gauge
    square wire
One heavy duty
    one-inch pin back
Temporary binding
    wire

5 Place one end of the remaining 6-inch piece of wire in the pin vise and hold the opposite end with the flat nose pliers. Twist the wire clockwise until the end in the pin vise breaks off (see fig. 2).

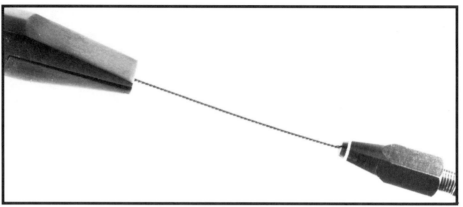

FIG. 2

6 Center the pin back on the center mark on the back of the bundle. Bind one side of the pin back to the bundle with temporary binding wire (see fig. 3).

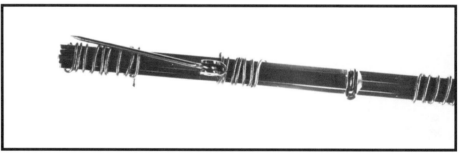

FIG. 3

7 Form one end of the twisted wire into a hook using the flat nose pliers (see fig. 4).

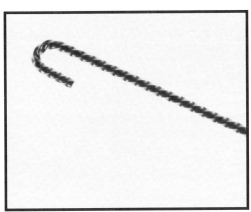

FIG. 4

8 Check your work against pattern 2.

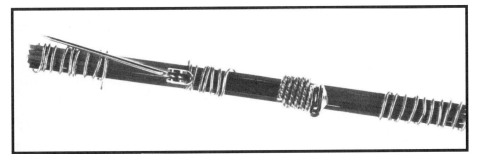

PATTERN 2

9 Place the hook in the twisted wire over the bundle and the pin back on the end opposite that which has the temporary binding wire. Hold the hook with the flat nose pliers and wrap three turns (see fig. 5).

FIG. 5

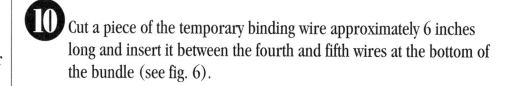

Note

If you decide to make a bar pin without the dangle, ignore steps 10 and 13

10 Cut a piece of the temporary binding wire approximately 6 inches long and insert it between the fourth and fifth wires at the bottom of the bundle (see fig. 6).

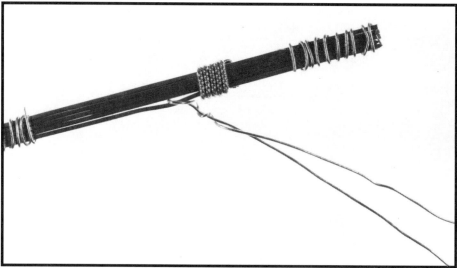

FIG. 6

11 Remove the temporary binding wire from the pin back. Bend another hook in your twisted wire and place it over the bundle and pin back. Hold the hook in place with the flat nose pliers and make three wraps in the direction opposite from those on the other side (see fig. 7).

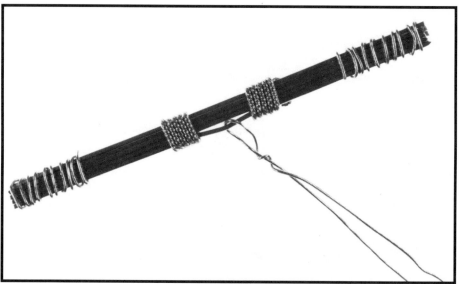

FIG.7

12 Check your work against pattern 3.

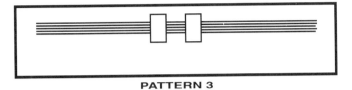

PATTERN 3

13 Using the flat nose pliers, grasp the end of the loop of temporary binding wire and pull down gently to separate the fourth and fifth wires enough to allow the tip of the round nose pliers between them. Insert the tip of the round nose pliers and carefully form the loop for the dangle (see fig. 8).

FIG. 8

14 Check the position of the outer wraps on pattern 4. Form another hook on your twisted wire, hold it in place with the flat nose pliers and make three wraps on the left-hand side of the bundle (see fig. 9). Repeat the operation on the right-hand side. Be certain to wrap in opposite directions.

FIG. 9

15 Check the position of your wraps against pattern 4.

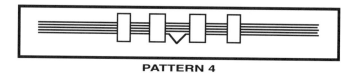

PATTERN 4

16 Remove the temporary binding wire from both ends of the bundle and fan the wires out. Hold the outer wrap with the flat nose pliers and, with the pin vise, twist the right-hand wires clockwise and the left-hand wires counterclockwise (see fig. 10).

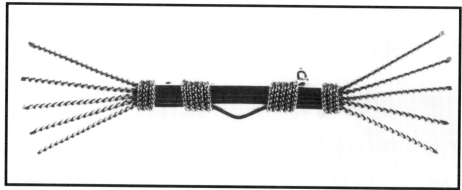

FIG. 10

17 Choose pattern 5A or 5B. Measure the bundle ends and cut to length.

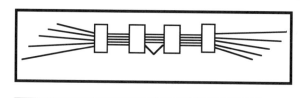

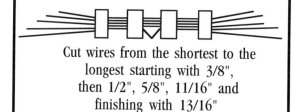

Cut wires from the shortest to the longest starting with 3/8", then 1/2", 5/8", 11/16" and finishing with 13/16"

PATTERNS 5A (TOP) AND 5B (BOTTOM)

18 File the cut ends with a Swiss file. Be sure to file the ends of the wrappings.and make certain to smooth the sharp spots. Polish the entire wire bundle with the polishing cloth.

19 Examine figures 11 and 12 and pick the design that most pleases you. Bend the scrolls with the round nose pliers beginning with the shortest wire and working toward the longest. Be sure that all parts of the pin are properly shaped and aligned, then give the piece a final polishing with the jeweler's cloth.

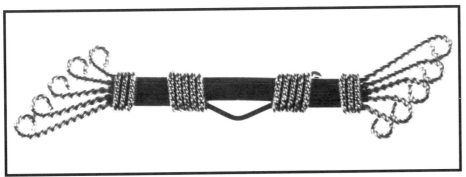

FIG. 11

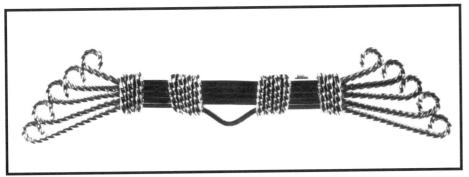

FIG. 12

20 If you made the bar with the dangle loop, hang your favorite charm from the loop, or make one of the other dangle projects to use on the bar. Most of all, have fun and use your creativity.

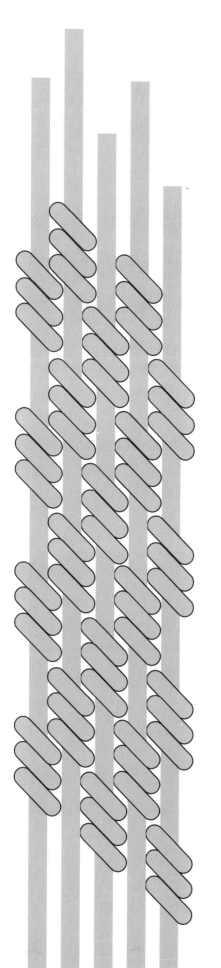

P R O J E C T 4

Spool Loom Chain

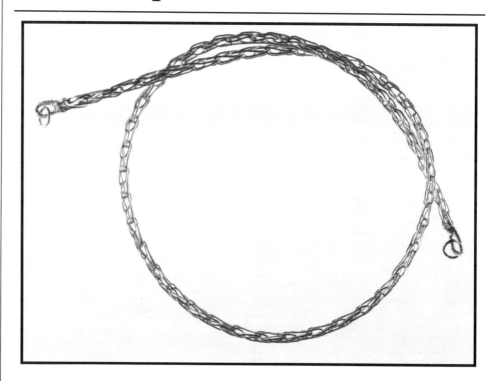

Although chain making is not specifically a wire wrapping technique, it is a relatively easy skill to learn and will give you the ability to make custom chains for your wire wrap projects. Because it is easy to learn and takes very few tools and materials, chain making is also a very good project for schools or youth groups.

Before you can begin the chain making project, you will need to make two special tools—a chain finishing board and a spool loom.

To make the finishing board, cut a 1/2-inch-thick block of hardwood 2 inches wide by 4 inches long and drill a double row of holes in these sizes: 5/16 inch, 1/4 inch, 3/16 inch, 7/32 inch, 5/32 inch, and 1/8 inch (refer to sketch 1 for the correct spacing).

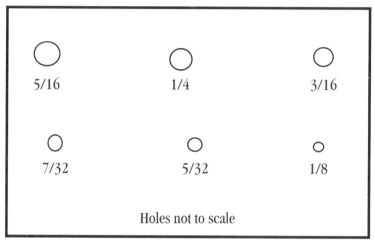

5/16 1/4 3/16

7/32 5/32 1/8

Holes not to scale

SKETCH 1

Countersink each hole slightly on both sides and sand the whole block smooth (see fig. 1 for the finished board.).

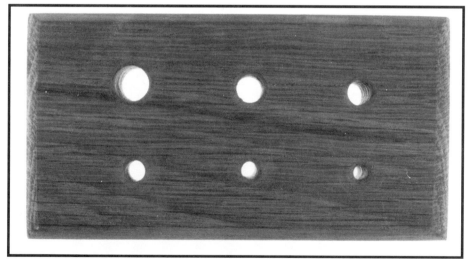

FIG. 1

TOOLS REQUIRED:
Chain nose pliers
Cutting pliers
Polishing cloth

SPECIAL TOOLS:
Spool loom
Finishing board
Tape measure
Medium crochet hook
1-inch finishing nails

MATERIALS REQUIRED:
One 1-ounce coil of
  24- or 26-gauge
  round wire
Two large jump rings
One lobster claw-style
  clasp

OPTIONAL MATERIALS:
Two beading style end
  cones

Note
If you have trouble finding the right size piece of wood, you may use a strip of 1/2-inch-thick hardwood 1 inch by 6 inches and drill a single row of holes.

The most difficult part of making the spool loom may be finding the spools. If you are lucky enough to have a packrat in the family, or if you can get into grandma's sewing basket, you may find a few spools. Craft stores often sell re-productions of spools for various projects, and this may be the avenue for you to take. If you cannot find spools, cut, or have someone cut for you, a few hardwood squares measuring 3/4 inch by 2 by 2 inches. Drill a 7/16-inch hole through the middle and follow the instructions for the spools below.

You will need at least two looms—one with three pins and one with four pins. In addition, you will need some one-inch finishing nails for the pins. On the first loom draw a triangle on the top with the points between 1/8 inch and 1/4 inch from the edge of the center hole (see fig. 2 on page 48).

Be careful to make all the markings the same distance from the edge of the center hole. Drive a finishing nail into the loom at each of the points on your triangle. Leave approximately 1/2 inch of each nail protruding (see sketch 2). On the top of the other loom, draw a square. Keep the points the same distance from the edge of the center hole as for the three-point loom. Drive the finishing nails in as you did on the first one.

3 pin loom	4 pin loom
3 pins set at 120 degrees to each other 1/8" from center hole	4 pins set at 90 degrees to each other 1/8" from center hole

SKETCH 2

Making the Chain

Special Instructions

1. One ounce of wire is enough to make several 16-inch chains.
2. When you pull the chain through the finishing board, the weave will tighten up and the chain will grow in length. Be sure to keep notes on the following items when you start making chains:
    - A. The number of pins on the loom
    - B. The wire gauge
    - C. The starting length of the chain
    - D. The finished length of the chain
3. With a four-pin loom and 24-gauge wire, a 14 1/2-inch unfinished chain will become a 16-inch finished chain.
4. If a wire should break during the weaving, twist the two ends together and cut off the excess as close to the twist as possible. The break will not be readily noticeable when the chain is finished. Of course, you can solder the break for a perfect job.
5. When showing your work, be sure to mention that the chains are woven from a single strand of wire. (The author once sold a chain made of sterling silver wire woven on a four-pin loom of 26-gauge wire to a customer who was so impressed with the flexibility and the subtle beauty of the work that she made the comment that it looked as if it had been woven from an angel's hair.)
6. Finally, be prepared to spend three to four hours per chain. Weaving wire is slow work, but remember: Good things take time and patience.

1 Uncoil a few feet of wire from your coil and rebind the coil to prevent tangling. CAUTION: DO NOT CUT THE WIRE. Insert the wire through the center hole of the loom until about four or five inches protrude from the bottom (see fig. 2).

FIG. 2

2 Wrap the wire around the pins on the loom once in a clockwise direction (see sketch 3).

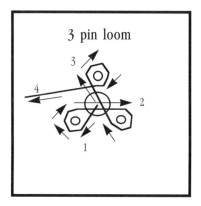

SKETCH 3

3 Continue the wrap around the next pin and over the top of the first loop (see fig. 3A.). Using the crochet hook, carefully pick up the bottom loop and lift it over the top loop (see fig. 3B.). Do not let the top loop come off the pin.

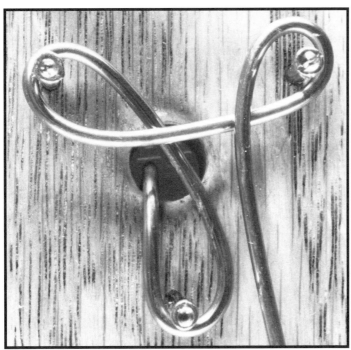

FIG. 3A

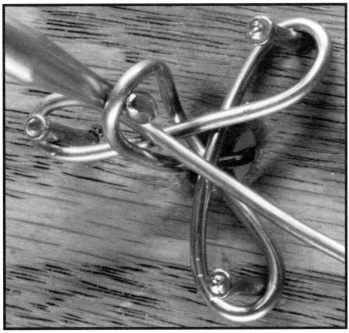

FIG. 3B.

4 Continue the procedure in step 3 until all the pins have one set of loops over the first set. Pull gently on the wire protruding from the bottom of the loom.

5 Continue the process of wrapping the loops around the pins, lifting the bottom loops over the top loops, and pulling down on the protruding wire. After a few minutes of this, the woven chain will begin to appear at the bottom of the center hole of the loom (see fig. 4).

FIG. 4

6 Continue weaving until you have the length of chain you wish. (Remember that the unfinished length will be shorter than the finished length.) At this point, you should cut the wire from the bulk coil. Leave four or five inches attached at the top of the chain (see fig. 5).

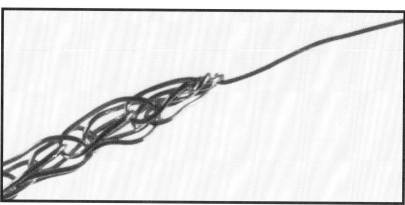

FIG. 5

7 Before lifting the loops off the pins, run the cut end of the wire through all the loops remaining on the loom to close the weave (see sketch 4).

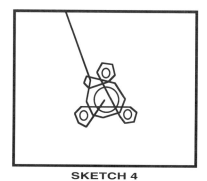

SKETCH 4

8 Lift the loops off the loom pins and, while pulling on the end strand, push the loops together to tie off the end of the weave (see fig. 6).

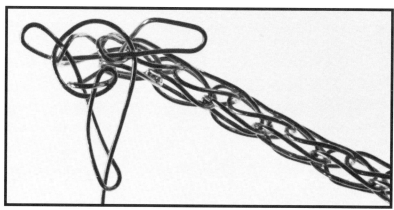

FIG. 6

9 Feed the end strand through the largest hole in the finishing board in which the chain will make contact. Pull the strand very gently with the chain nose pliers until the weave starts to come out the back of the board. (Pulling too hard will cause the strand to break, so be very gentle. Whenever possible, pull on the weave and not on the end strand.) Grasp the weave with your fingers and continue to pull it through the board (see fig. 7).

FIG. 7

10 Pull the chain through the hole five to ten times, then move to the next smaller hole. Repeat the process until you have pulled the chain through three holes. Pull it through each hole five to ten times to tighten the weave. Trying to pull it through more than three sizes of holes will probably cause the end strand to break. Three holes should produce a fine chain.

11 To finish a chain end, use the chain nose pliers to pull gently on the longest loop. When the loop is the size you desire, wrap the end strand around the base of the loops several times and feed it through the weave. Wrap two or three turns around the weave and cut off the excess wire (see fig. 8). Repeat the process with the other end.

Note
For optional end finishing using beading end cones, see sketch 5.

FIG. 8

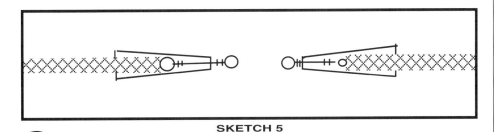

SKETCH 5

12 Polish the chain by pulling it through your polishing cloth repeatedly. Work from both ends and twist the chain slightly after each pass. This will both polish the chain and loosen up the weave.

13 Install the jump rings and the clasp and the project is complete.

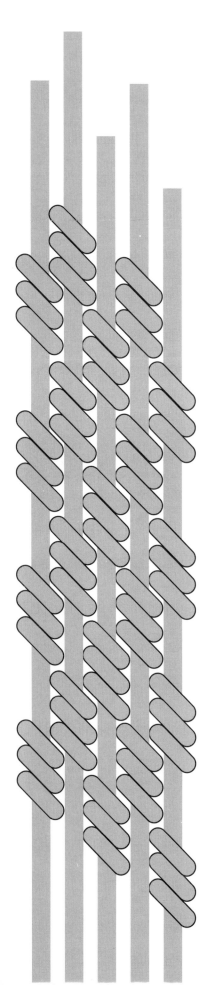

5

A Mixed Wire Ribbon Pendant

This project is designed to demonstrate the use of different wire shapes in combination. The pendant is best worn on a long chain of substantial thickness, such as one of the spool loom chains. The pendant also looks great on the Bar Dangle Charm Pin.

1 Cut two 6-inch lengths of 20-gauge square wire and one 6-inch piece of 14-gauge half-round wire.

2 Lay out the 14-gauge half-round wire and straighten it. Lay a piece of the 20-gauge square wire on each side of the half-round wire. Bind each end of the bundle with the temporary binding wire (see fig. 1).

TOOLS REQUIRED:
Pin vise
Pliers
Swiss file set
Polishing cloth

OPTIONAL TOOL:
Ring mandrel

MATERIALS REQUIRED:
12 inches of 20-gauge
  square wire
14 inches of 14-gauge
  half-round wire
One 30x22mm cabo-
  chon
Temporary binding
  wire

FIG. 1

3 Check your work against pattern 1.

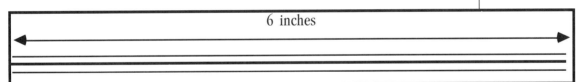

6 inches

PATTERN 1

4 With the remaining piece of 14-gauge half-round wire, form a hook for the wrapping (see fig. 2).

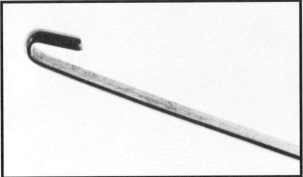

FIG. 2

5 Check your work against pattern 2

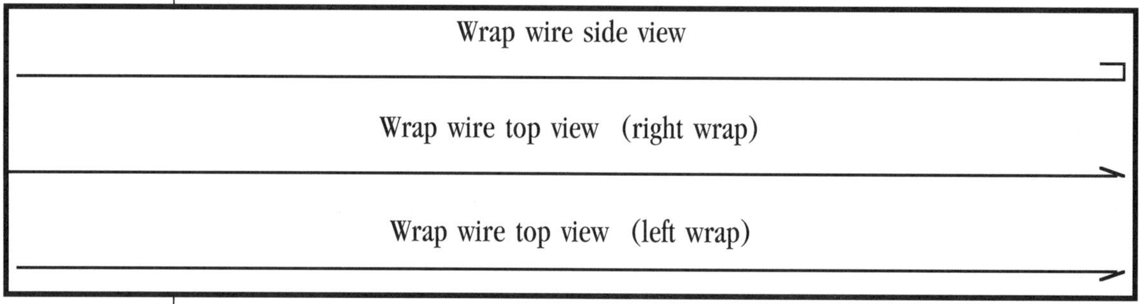

Wrap wire side view

Wrap wire top view (right wrap)

Wrap wire top view (left wrap)

PATTERN 2

6 Place the hook over the bundle just to the right of the center point, hold it with the flat nose pliers, and make two wraps toward the end of the bundle. Form another hook and repeat the process on the left side of the center point (see fig. 3).

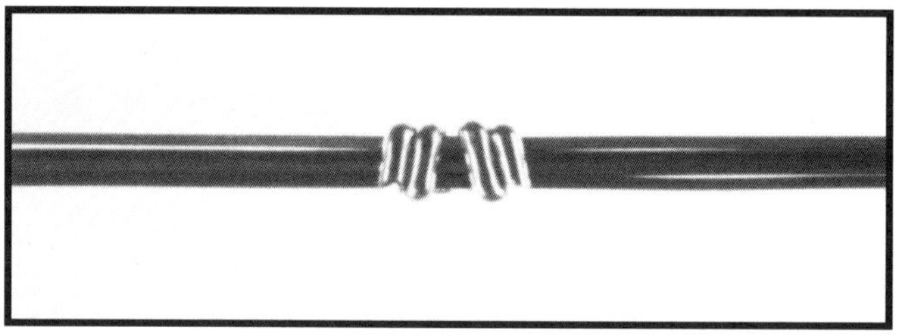

FIG. 3

7 Check your work against pattern 3.

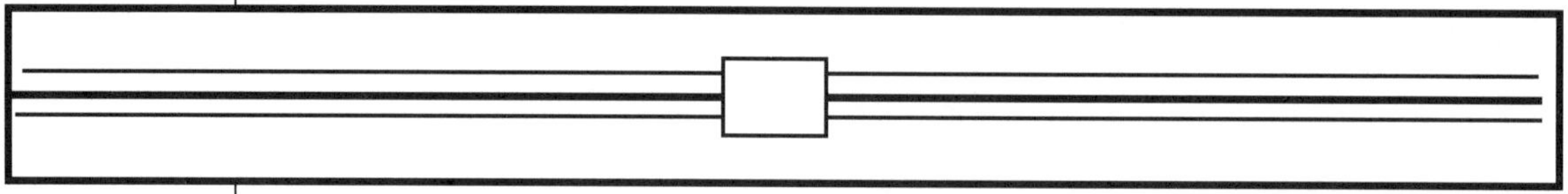

PATTERN 3

8 Remove the temporary binding wire and fan the front wires out. Hold the center wrap with the flat nose pliers and use the pin vise to twist the right side square wire clockwise and the left side square wire counterclockwise (see fig. 4).

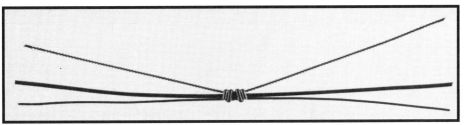

FIG. 4

Note
Do not twist the half-round wire or the back square wire.

9 Rewrap the bundle with the temporary binding wire. Check pattern 4 for the wrap positions, and wrap the bundle with the half-round wire three turns on each side of center. Wrap one side to the right and the other to the left.

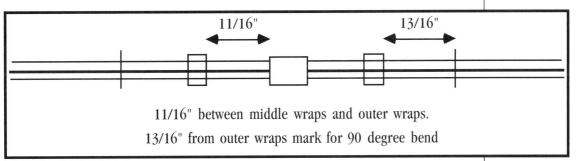

11/16"   13/16"

11/16" between middle wraps and outer wraps.
13/16" from outer wraps mark for 90 degree bend

PATTERN 4

10 File the cut ends of the wrappings with one of the Swiss files to eliminate the sharp spots. Polish the bundle with the jeweler's cloth.

11 Form the wire bundle around your cabochon or around a ring mandrel at ring size 10.

12 Check your work against pattern 5.

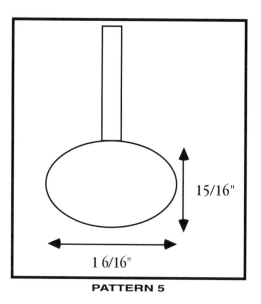

15/16"

1 6/16"

PATTERN 5

13 Lace the bundle ends together with the temporary binding wire (see fig. 5).

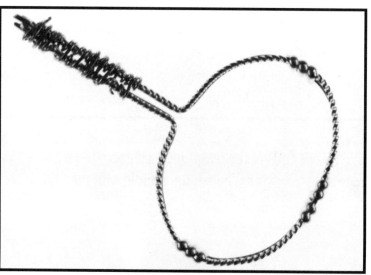

FIG. 5

14 Form another hook with the 14-gauge half-round wire. Place the hook over the bundle as close to the bend as possible. Hold the hook with the flat nose pliers and wrap three turns toward the bundle ends. Remove the temporary binding wire and fan out the bundle ends (see fig. 6).

FIG. 6

15 Using the flat nose pliers, carefully form the back stone prongs on the back wire of the pendant (see fig.7).

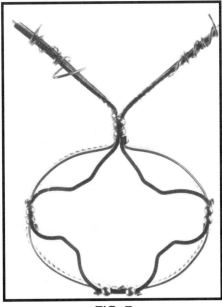

FIG. 7

16 Check your work against pattern 6.

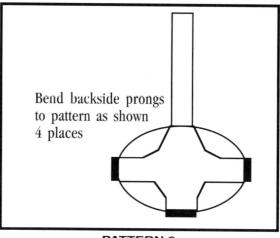

Bend backside prongs
to pattern as shown
4 places

PATTERN 6

17 Remove the temporary binding wire from the top of the bundle. Hold the top wrap with the flat nose pliers and twist the square wires with the pin vise. Twist the right wire clockwise and the left wire counterclockwise (see fig. 8).

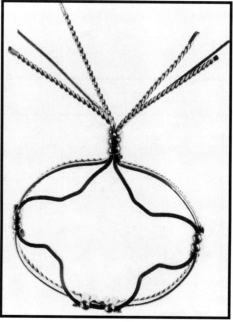

FIG. 8

18 Hold the top wrapping with the chain nose pliers. Using the flat nose pliers, twist the half-round wires two to three turns. Twist the right wire clockwise and the left wire counterclockwise, which gives the half-round wire a ribbon effect (see fig. 9).

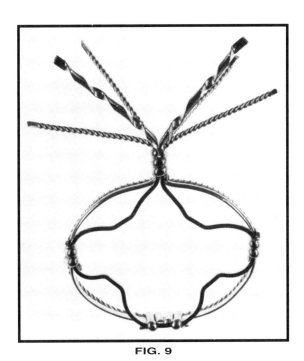

FIG. 9

19 Refer to pattern 7 for the lengths of the top wires and cut them to the correct lengths. Smooth the ends of the wires with a Swiss file.

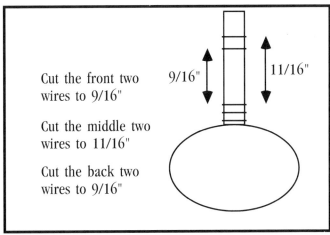

Cut the front two wires to 9/16"

Cut the middle two wires to 11/16"

Cut the back two wires to 9/16"

9/16"   11/16"

PATTERN 7

20 Place the stone in the pendant and close the cage by carefully forming the front prongs with the flat nose pliers (see fig.10).

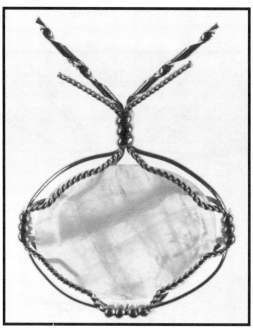

FIG. 10

21 With the round nose pliers, carefully bend the scrolls in the front two square wires and in the half-round wires. Form the back two wires into the dangle loop by scrolling them toward each other and overlapping them (see fig. 11).

FIG. 11

Form the dangle bail with 14-gauge half-round wire (see fig. 12).

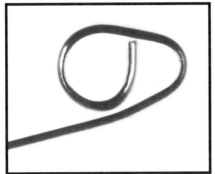

FIG. 12

 Check your work against pattern 8.

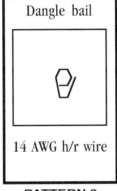

Dangle bail

14 AWG h/r wire

PATTERN 8

 Attach the bail to the pendant's dangle loop and give the project a final polishing with the jeweler's cloth.

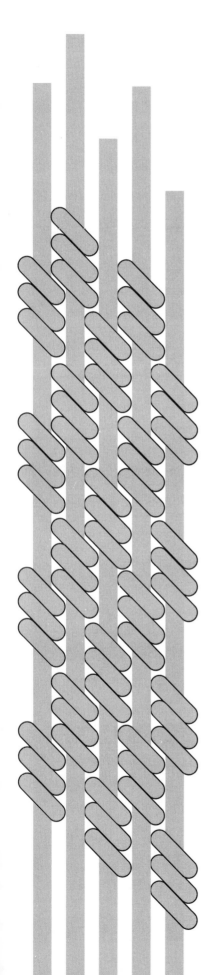

PROJECT 6

Drop Dangle Cabochon Earrings

Meant for a lifetime of wear, these earrings have a wonderful antique look, a nice weight and sturdy construction. They make a fine accessory with the other cabochon projects. A special benefit of the design is that you can make just one earring to wear as a pendant.

1 Cut four 4-inch pieces of the 20-gauge square wire and two 6-inch pieces of the 16-gauge half-round wire.

2 Using two 4-inch square wires and one 4-inch half-round wire, make a bundle with the half-round wire in the middle. Bind the ends with temporary binding wire and mark the center point of the bundle (see fig. 1). Repeat the procedure for the second earring.

FIG. 1

3 Check your work against pattern 1.

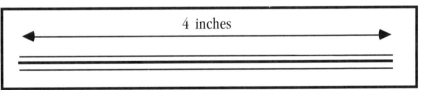

4 inches

PATTERN 1

TOOLS REQUIRED:
Pin vise
Pliers
Swiss file set
Polishing cloth

OPTIONAL TOOL:
Ring mandrel

MATERIALS REQUIRED:
16 inches of 20-gauge
  square wire
20 inches of 16-gauge
  half-round wire
Two 18x13 mm
  matched cabochons
One pair earwire
  hooks
Temporary binding
  wire

4 Form a hook on the end of the remaining piece of half-round wire (see fig. 2).

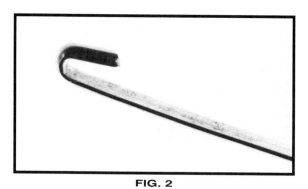

FIG. 2

5 Check your work against pattern 2.

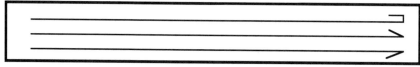

PATTERN 2

6 Place the hook over the bundle next to the center point, hold it with the flat nose pliers, and make two wraps of the half-round wire to the right of center. Form another hook and repeat the process on the left side of center. Be sure to wrap one wire to the right and the other to the left (see fig. 3). Repeat the procedure for the second earring.

FIG. 3

7 Check your work against pattern 3.

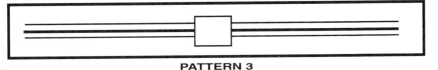

PATTERN 3

8 Remove the temporary binding wire from the bundle ends and fan the front wires out. Hold the center wrap with the flat nose pliers and, with the pin vise, twist the right square wire clockwise, and the left square wire counterclockwise (see fig. 4). Repeat the process for the other earring.

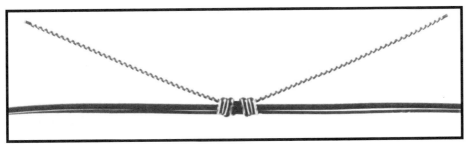

FIG. 4

9 Close the wires and rewrap the bundle ends with the temporary binding wire. Check pattern 4 for the placement of the next wraps. Form another hook in your half-round wire and place it on the right side of the bundle at the proper location. Make two wraps to the right. Repeat the wrap on the left side, making sure to wrap to the left. Follow the same procedure for the other earring.

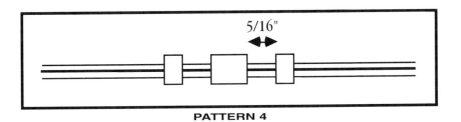

5/16"

PATTERN 4

Note

Do not twist the half-round wire or the back square wires.

10 File the ends of all the wrappings with a Swiss file. Be sure to eliminate all of the sharp spots. Polish both of the bundles.

11 Begin forming the wire bundle around your cabochon or around a ring mandrel at position 1 (see fig. 5). Repeat the process with the second earring.

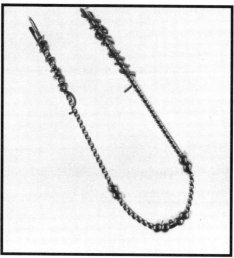

FIG. 5

12 Check your work against pattern 5.

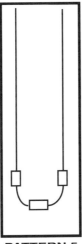

PATTERN 5

13 Bring the ends of the bundle together and wrap them with the temporary binding wire. Form another hook in your half-round wire and place it as close to the top bend as possible. Wrap two turns toward the top of the bundle (see fig. 6). Repeat the process for the other earring. Check your work against pattern 6.

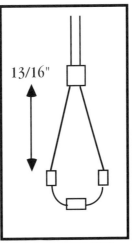

13/16"

FIG. 6 (LEFT) AND PATTERN 6 (RIGHT)

14 With the flat nose pliers, carefully form the stone prongs on the back wires of each earring in four places (see fig. 7).

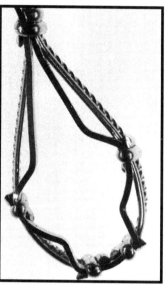

FIG. 7

15 Check your work against pattern 7.

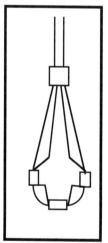

PATTERN 7

16 Remove the temporary binding wire at the top of the earring. With the pin vise, twist the square wires. Twist the right wires clockwise and the left wires counterclockwise (see fig. 8).

FIG. 8

17 Check the dimensions on pattern 8 and cut the top wires to length. File the ends of the wires with a Swiss file to remove all sharp spots. Repeat the operations on the second earring.

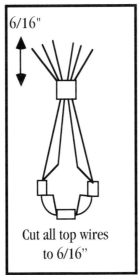

6/16"

Cut all top wires
to 6/16"

PATTERN 8

18 Place the stone in the earring and close the cage by carefully forming the front prongs in four places with the flat nose pliers (see fig. 9).

FIG. 9

19 With the round nose pliers, carefully form the scrolls in the front square wires and the middle half-round wires. Form the dangle loop in the back square wires by scrolling them toward each other and overlapping the loops (see fig. 10). Repeat the process on the other earring.

FIG. 10

20 Give the earrings a final polish with the jeweler's cloth and attach the wire hooks onto the dangle loops.

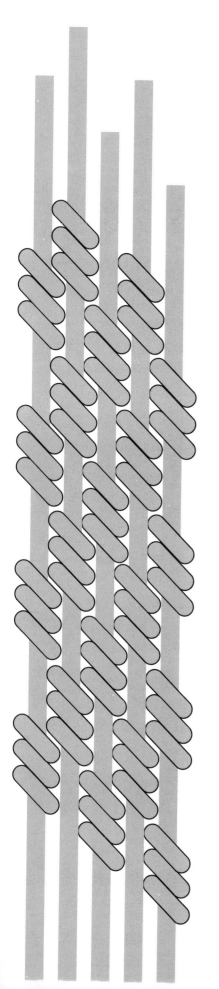

PROJECT 7

A Wide Band Pearl Ring

This ring is a classic example of wire wrapping at its best. Using twisted square wire for the wrappings results in an antique look. Use a half-round wire instead of the twisted square wire for a modern look. A pearl ring is an old-fashioned favorite that is prized today. This ring can be worn alone or matched with the pearl drop earrings in project 2.

The patterns for the pearl ring are designed for a size 6 ring, but other sizes are easily made simply by adding or subtracting wraps. Each 3/32 of an inch (between 1/16 inch and 2/16 inch) equals one ring size.

When using a natural pearl, use gold-filled wire. This will make the project a real beauty and add a great deal to the value. If you do use a natural pearl, be sure to avoid harsh abrasive cleaners or cleaners with even mild acids, since these will destroy the pearl's luster.

1 Cut three 4-inch pieces of 20-gauge square wire and bind them together with the temporary binding wire (see fig. 1).

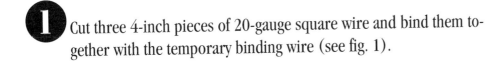

FIGURE 1

2 Check your work with pattern 1

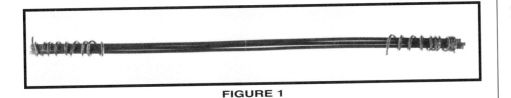

4 inches

PATTERN 1

3 Place one end of the remaining square wire in the pin vise. Hold the opposite end with the flat nose pliers and twist until the end in the vise breaks off. Because this wire is so long, the end nearest the pin vise will have a tighter twist than the opposite end when the break occurs. To solve this problem, reverse the ends and continue twisting until the pin vise end breaks again. Be sure to keep twisting in the same direction, or you will unwind your initial twists (see fig. 2).

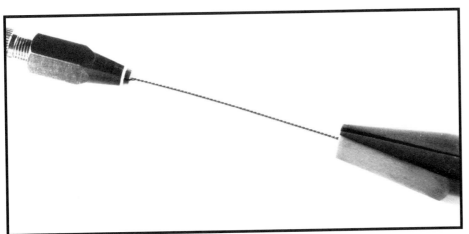

FIG. 2

4 Form a hook on one end of the twisted wire (see fig. 3.).

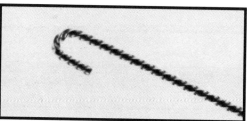

FIG. 3

5 Check your work against pattern 2

Length should be about 20 inches

Side view

Top view

PATTERN 2

6 Place the hook over the temporarily wrapped bundle about one inch from one end. Hold the hook with the flat nose pliers and wrap toward the other end of the bundle. When you have wrapped approximately 2 1/2 inches (check your work with pattern 3), cut the twisted wire off on the same side of the bundle as the starting wrap.

2 1/2 inches

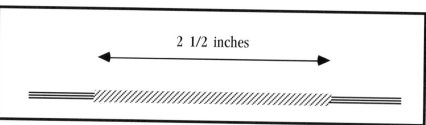

PATTERN 3

7 Remove the temporary binding wires and fan out the wires on both ends. With the pin vise, twist each end wire 10 to 12 times (see fig. 4.).

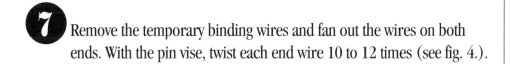

FIG. 4

8 Check pattern 4 and cut the end wires to the dimensions shown.

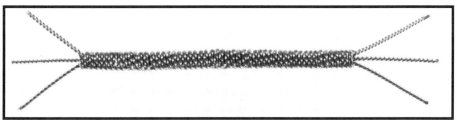

11/16"   11/16"

PATTERN 4

9 Scroll the cut end wires in five places (see fig. 5.).

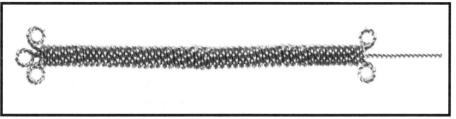

FIG. 5

10 Bend the remaining end wire upward at a 90-degree angle (see fig. 6). This becomes the pearl mounting post that locks the ring together.

FIG. 6

11 Form the bundle slowly and carefully around the ring mandrel. Insert the pearl post through the scrolled loop on the opposite end of the bundle. Hold the post with the flat nose pliers and carefully move the ring to the 6 position on the mandrel. Be careful not to unroll the scroll around the post, and be sure to keep the post at a 90 degree angle (see fig. 7).

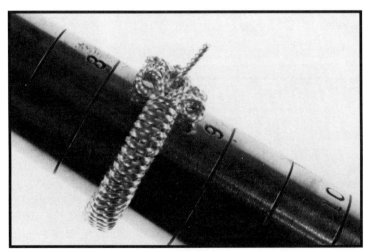

FIG. 7

12 Insert the post into the pearl and check the depth of the drilling. Cut off a snippet of the post at a time until the pearl rests against the loop. Fasten the pearl to the post with 5-minute epoxy. Leave the ring on the mandrel for 12 to 24 hours to be certain that the epoxy is hardened.

13 Check the four outer scrolled loops and straighten if necessary. Polish the ring with the polishing cloth and the project is complete.

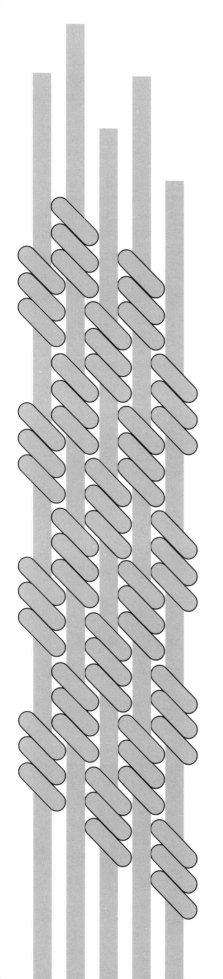

PROJECT 8

A Rope Border Coin Holder

Coins have been used as jewelry since ancient times, and are as popular today as ever. This project is an updated version of an old-fashioned favorite that you can craft for yourself. If you do not have a good example of a buffalo or liberty head nickel, you can find one at a coin shop for a few dollars. All that is needed is a coin that shows nice detail. Putting a mint coin in jewelry is unnecessary, since it will not remain mint for long.

While the coin may be used as is, a little polishing compound will remove light scratches. Some silver oxidizer, available at lapidary and jewelry supply stores, will give it the look of an old coin.

Either gold-filled or silver wire work fine with this project.

1 Lay out four 5-inch pieces of 20-gauge square wire into a bundle and bind the ends with temporary binding wire. Mark the center point of the bundle (see fig. 1).

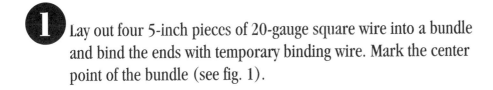

FIG. 1

2 Check your work against pattern 1.

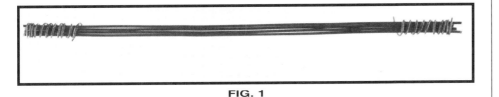

5 inches

PATTERN 1

3 Place one end of the remaining wire in the pin vise, hold the opposite end with the flat nose pliers, and twist until the end in the vise breaks off (see fig. 2).

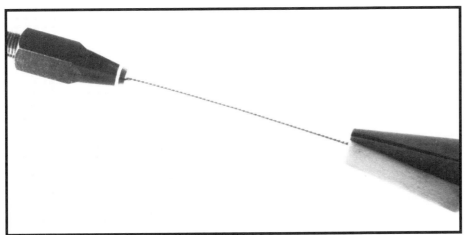

FIG. 2

TOOLS REQUIRED:
Pin vise
Pliers
Swiss file set
Polishing cloth
Ring mandrel

MATERIALS REQUIRED:
28 inches of 20-gauge square wire
One inch of 14-gauge half-round wire
One buffalo or liberty nickel
Temporary binding wire

4 With the flat nose pliers, form a hook on one end of the twisted wire (see fig. 3).

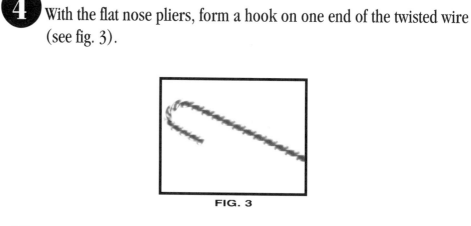

FIG. 3

5 Check your work against pattern 2.

PATTERN 2

6 Place the hook in the twisted wire over the four-wire bundle just to the right of the center mark. Be sure that the long end of the twisted wire is on the top of the bundle. Hold the hook to the bundle with the flat nose pliers and wrap seven turns to the right. Cut off the twisted wire with the last wrap on the bottom of the bundle. Form another hook and repeat the operation on the other side of the bundle. Be sure to wrap to the left. Crimp the wraps with the flat nose pliers (see fig. 4).

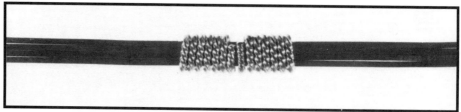

FIG. 4

7 Check your work against pattern 3.

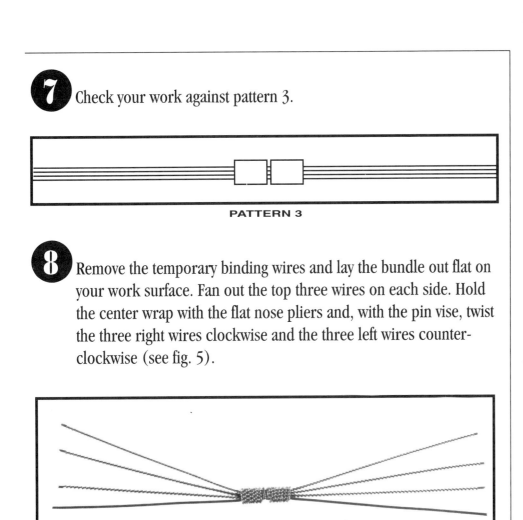

PATTERN 3

8 Remove the temporary binding wires and lay the bundle out flat on your work surface. Fan out the top three wires on each side. Hold the center wrap with the flat nose pliers and, with the pin vise, twist the three right wires clockwise and the three left wires counter-clockwise (see fig. 5).

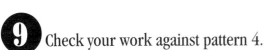

FIG. 5

9 Check your work against pattern 4.

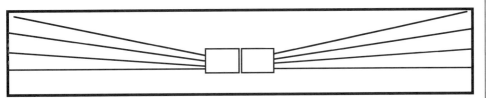

PATTERN 4

Note

Do not be alarmed if the coin does not fit. The sizing process will remedy this as you progress.

10 Reform the bundle and rewrap the ends with the temporary binding wire. Check pattern 5 and mark the positions for the 90 degree bends.

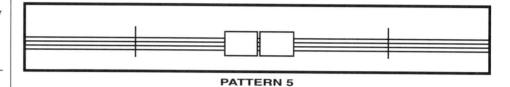

PATTERN 5

11 File smooth the cut ends with the Swiss file and polish the project.

12 Place the middle mark on the bundle at step 10 1/2 on the ring mandrel and begin to form the bundle around the mandrel. Let the ends of the bundle cross each other at the top. With the flat nose pliers, bend the bundle ends up 90 degrees at the markings you made in step 10. Bind the ends of the bundle together with temporary binding wire (see fig. 6).

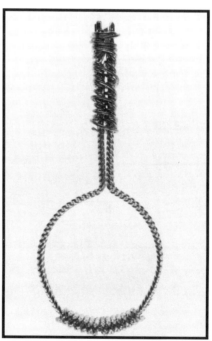

FIG. 6

13 Form another hook on your twisted wire, hold it as close as possible to the bends in the bundle with the flat nose pliers, and wrap three turns upward toward the bundle ends. Cut the wrap wire off on the back of the bundle (see fig. 7).

Note
Do not crimp the wrap yet. There will be some wire slippage during the final sizing process.

FIG. 7

14 Slide the holder onto the ring mandrel and slowly work it upward toward the 11 1/2 ring size. When you near this point, remove the holder, turn it around, and repeat the process. Keep working in this manner and checking the fit of the coin frequently. The coin must fit the holder loop very snugly, since friction keeps it in place. Do not size the holder past the 11 1/2 mark or the coin will be too loose. Orient the coin in the direction you wish and snap it in place. Be certain it fits exactly the way you want, since adjustments beyond this are virtually impossible. When you are satisfied with the orientation, crimp the top bundle wrappings with the flat nose pliers (see fig. 8).

FIG. 8

15 After the coin is firmly in its holder, form the back prongs. Gripping the back wires at the bottom wrappings with the flat nose pliers, pull gently toward the center of the holder. Use the same procedure for the top prongs (see fig. 9).

FIG. 9

16 Check your work against pattern 6.

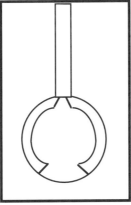

PATTERN 6

17 Form the front prongs using the chain nose pliers. Grip the wires in the same places as you did for the back prongs, but move the wires just enough so that the prong covers just the edge of the coin. This allows the maximum amount of the coin face to show (see fig. 10).

FIG. 10

18 Check your work against pattern 7.

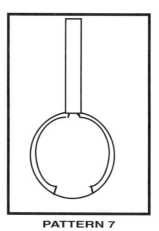

PATTERN 7

19 Remove the temporary binding wire from the top of the bundle. With the pin vise, twist the remaining right wire clockwise and the remaining left wire counterclockwise (see fig. 11).

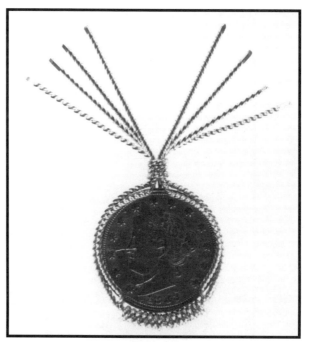

FIG. 11

20 Cut the top wires to the lengths illustrated in pattern 8. File the cut ends with a Swiss file.

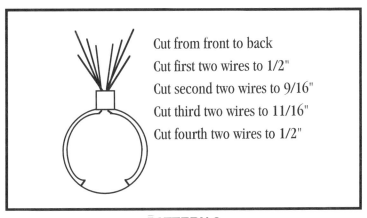

Cut from front to back
Cut first two wires to 1/2"
Cut second two wires to 9/16"
Cut third two wires to 11/16"
Cut fourth two wires to 1/2"

PATTERN 8

21 Using just the last 1/8 inch of the tip of the round nose pliers, carefully bend the scrolls on the front two wires. Repeat the process
with the second set of wires, and finally scroll the third set. Form
the back two wires into the dangle loop by scrolling them toward
each other and then overlapping them (see fig. 12).

FIG. 12

22 Form the dangle bail from a piece of half-round 14-gauge wire and
install it on the dangle bail loops. Close the bail and give the project
a final polishing with the jeweler's cloth.

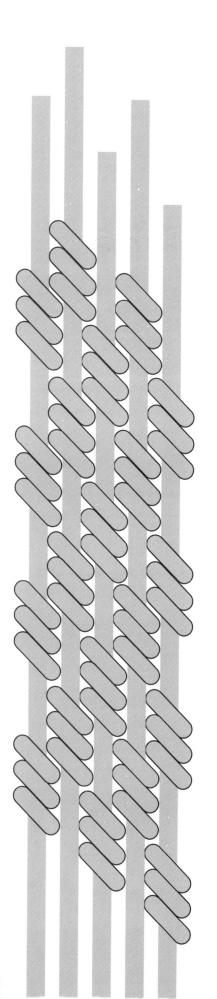

PROJECT 9

Four Simple Earring Styles

These earrings make great projects for youngsters or for the wire worker who wants a relatively inexpensive way to stock up on a ladies' earring collection. All four styles can be made from just one strand of 6mm beads. One 16-inch strand usually contains 68 beads—plenty for these projects with lots left over. These strands can be purchased for a few dollars each, depending on the type of material. Similarly, the fishhook earwires are very inexpensive, especially when bought in bulk. If you cannot find the fishhook wires, however, earwires or ball studs with a dangle loop work as well.

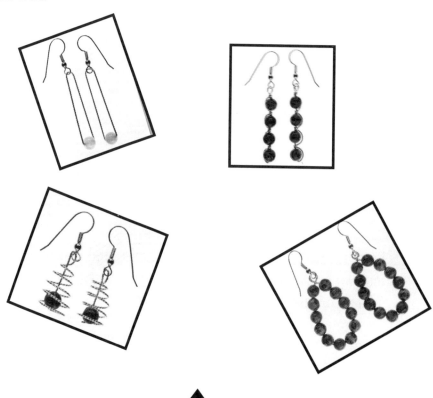

Style A

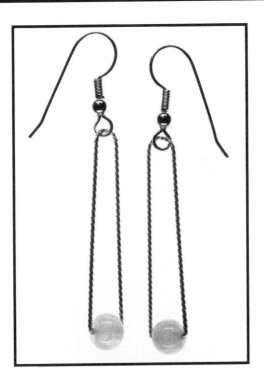

TOOLS REQUIRED:
Pin vise
Pliers
Swiss file set
Polishing cloth
Ring mandrel

MATERIALS REQUIRED:
6 inches of 22-gauge
   square wire
Two 6mm full round-
   drilled beads
One pair of fishhook
   dangle earwires
5-minute epoxy

1 Cut one 6 1/2-inch piece of 22-gauge square wire. With the pin vise and the flat nose pliers, twist the wire until the end in the pin vise breaks off (see fig. 1).

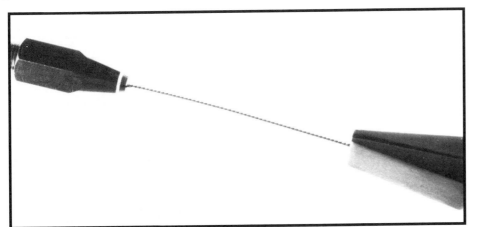

FIGURE 1

2 Polish the wire with the polishing cloth, being careful not to bend the wire. Cut the wire into two 3-inch pieces and file the cut ends with a Swiss file.

3 Check pattern 1 and bend both of the wires to shape using the round nose and flat nose pliers.

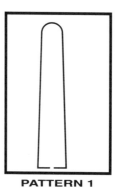

PATTERN 1

4 Check the fit of the beads, then bond them in place with the 5-minute epoxy (see fig. 2).

FIG. 2

5 Check your work against pattern 2.

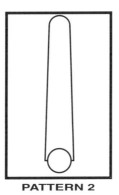

PATTERN 2

6 Attach the fishhook dangle earwires to the drops (see fig. 3).

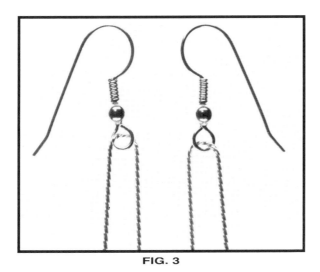

FIG. 3

7 Close the earwire dangle loops with the round nose pliers, and the project is complete.

TOOLS REQUIRED:
Pin vise
Pliers
Swiss file set
Polishing cloth

MATERIALS REQUIRED:
Ten inches of
    22-gauge square
    wire
Two 6mm round
    drilled beads
One pair of fishhook
    dangle earwires
5-minute epoxy

Style B

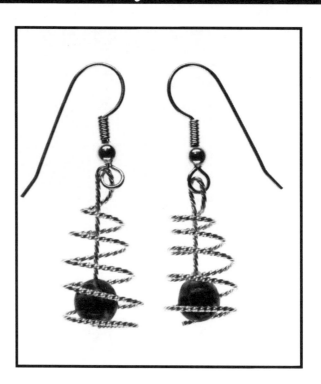

1 Cut one 10 1/2-inch piece of 22-gauge square wire. With the flat nose pliers and the pin vise, twist the wire until the end in the pin vise breaks off (see style A, fig. 1).

2 Polish the wire with the polishing cloth, being careful not to bend the wire during polishing. Cut the wire into two 5-inch pieces. File the cut ends with a Swiss file.

3 Form the spirals by placing 13/16 inch of the wire into the jaws of the chain nose pliers, slowly bending it around the outside of the pliers jaws in a downward spiral so that the wire held in the jaws of the pliers is inside the spiral (see fig. 1).

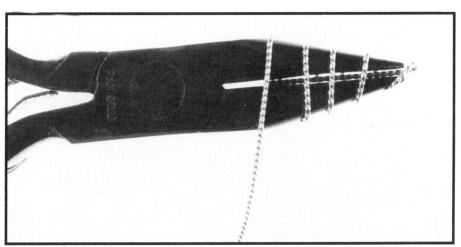

FIG. 1

4 Straighten and align the spirals and check your work against pattern 1.

PATTERN 1

5 Check the fit of the beads, then bond them with the 5-minute epoxy (see fig. 2).

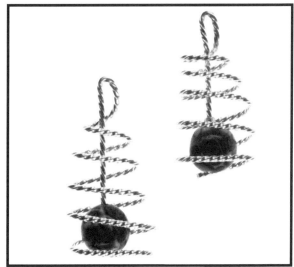

FIG. 2

6 Check your work against pattern 2.

PATTERN 2

7 Attach the fishhook dangle earwires to the drops (see fig. 3).

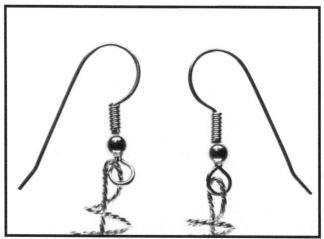

FIG. 3

8 Close the earwire dangle loops with the round nose pliers and the project is complete.

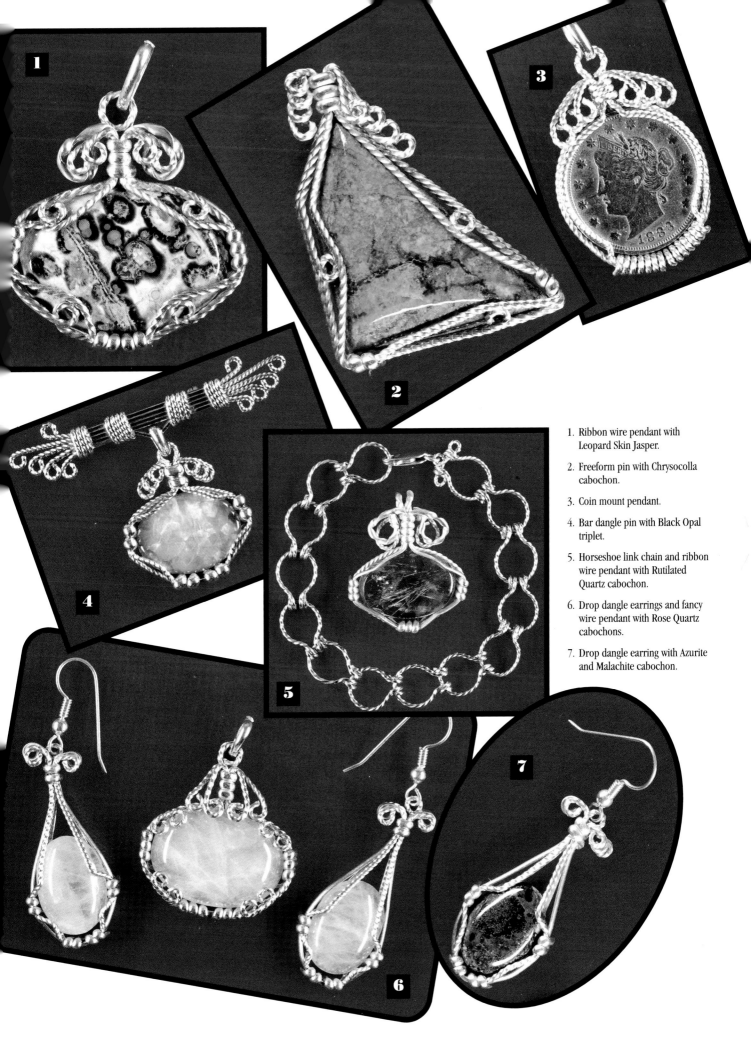

1. Ribbon wire pendant with Leopard Skin Jasper.

2. Freeform pin with Chrysocolla cabochon.

3. Coin mount pendant.

4. Bar dangle pin with Black Opal triplet.

5. Horseshoe link chain and ribbon wire pendant with Rutilated Quartz cabochon.

6. Drop dangle earrings and fancy wire pendant with Rose Quartz cabochons.

7. Drop dangle earring with Azurite and Malachite cabochon.

1. Spool loom chain and Drusy Quartz freeform pendant.

2. Eight-prong ring with Malachite cabochon.

3. Prongless twist cabochon ring with Linde Star stone.

4. Cage pendant with Fire Opal.

5. Double end pendant with Picture Jasper.

6. Cage pendant with Bullseye Malachite cabochon.

7. Cage pendant with Abalone shell.

8. Freeform pendant with Tourmaline in Quartz.

Style C

TOOLS REQUIRED:
Pin vise
Pliers
Swiss file set
Polishing cloth

MATERIALS REQUIRED:
12 inches of 22-gauge
    square wire
Eight 6mm round
    drilled beads
One pair of fishhook
    dangle earwires

1 Cut one piece of 22-gauge square wire 12 1/2 inches long. With the pin vise and the flat nose pliers, twist the wire until the end in the pin vise breaks off (see style A, fig. 1).

2 Polish the wire with the polishing cloth, being careful not to bend the wire. Cut the wire into two 6-inch pieces and file the cut ends with a Swiss file.

3 Form a 90-degree bend in each wire two inches from the end. Place one of the beads on the short end of the wire. Form the long end of the wire around the bead and make two wraps around the wire protruding from the other end of the bead (see fig. 1).

FIG. 1

4 Place another bead above the first and repeat the process until four beads are in place (see fig. 2).

FIG. 2

5 Check your work against pattern 1.

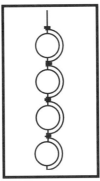

PATTERN 1

6 After wrapping the wire at the top of the fourth bead, cut off the excess wire and file the cut end with a Swiss file.

7 Clip the protruding wire to 1/2 inch. Form a loop in the protruding wire and turn it so that the wire formed around the beads is in the back where it will not show (see fig. 3).

FIG. 3

8 Check your work against pattern 2.

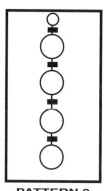

PATTERN 2

9 Attach the fishhook dangle earwires to the drops (see fig. 4).

FIG. 4

10 Close the fishhook dangle earwire loops with the round nose pliers and the project is complete.

Style D

TOOLS REQUIRED:
Pin vise
Pliers
Swiss file set
Polishing cloth

MATERIALS REQUIRED:
8 inches of 22-gauge
   square wire
Eight 6mm round
   drilled beads
One pair of fishhook
   dangle earwires

1 Cut one piece of 22-gauge square wire 8 1/2 inches long. With the pin vise and the flat nose pliers, twist the wire until the end in the pin vise breaks off (see style A, fig. 1).

2 Polish the wire with the polishing cloth, being careful not to bend the wire while polishing. Cut the wire into two 4-inch pieces. File the cut ends with a Swiss file.

3 Form a small loop on one end of each wire and slide 12 beads on each (see fig. 1).

FIG. 1

4 Form a second small loop on the opposite end to hold the beads in place (see fig. 2).

FIG. 2

5 Check your work against pattern 1.

PATTERN 1

6 Form the wire into a drop with both of the small loops overlapping (see fig. 3).

FIG. 3

7 Check your work against pattern 2.

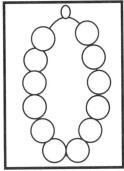

PATTERN 2

8 Attach the fishhook dangle earwires to the drops (see fig. 4).

FIG. 4

9 Close the fishhook dangle earwire loops with the round nose pliers and the project is complete.

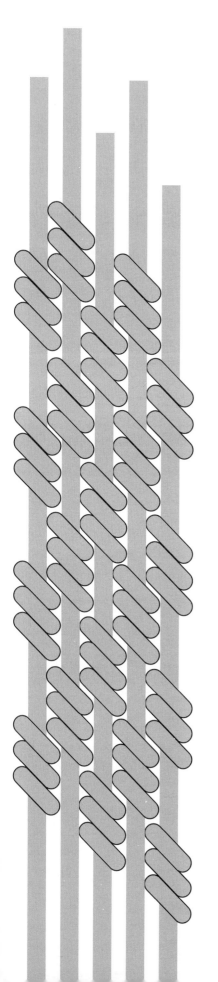

10

A Prongless Twist Cabochon Ring

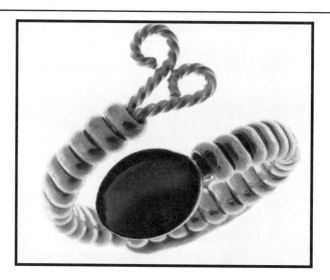

This is the only project in the book that requires some soldering in its construction. The soldering is very simple, however, and is easily accomplished without a torch. Of course, if you have a torch and the skill required to use it, do so by all means. Don't be put off if you don't, however, since the simplest little pencil-type soldering iron is more than adequate for this job.

This ring is perfect for displaying stones with cat's eyes, stars, or fire, because there are no prongs to cover up or detract from the stone's uniqueness. Although these stones are recommended, any stone benefits from this mount.

The sterling silver bezel cups come in a wide variety of styles and sizes; and although this ring uses a cup with a smooth border, the sawtooth design is acceptable. The desired size for the cup on this ring is 6X8mm, but 6mm round, 8mm round, 7X5mm oval, and 8X10mm oval cups will also work. Simply choose the one that pleases you the most.

Finally, this ring style is very easy to make. If you have struggled with some of the more complex ring styles, you will really appreciate this one.

1 Cut two 4-inch pieces of 20-gauge square wire. Match up one end of the two wires and bind both ends of the bundle with the temporary binding wire. Leave 1/2 inch of wire clear beyond the binding on one end (see fig. 1).

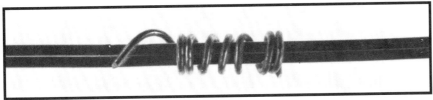

FIG. 1

2 File the matched ends with a Swiss file to remove sharp spots or burrs. Make sure that the ends are flat and even.

3 Check pattern 1 for the location of the bezel cup. Follow the instructions for the Staybrite solder and apply flux to the underside of the bezel cup and the matched ends of the wire bundle. Apply a small amount of solder to the tip of the pencil soldering iron and solder the cup to the matched ends of the bundle (see fig. 2).

PATTERN 1

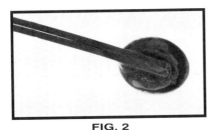

FIG. 2

TOOLS REQUIRED:
Pin vise
Pliers
Swiss file set
Polishing cloth
Ring mandrel
Pencil soldering iron

MATERIALS REQUIRED:
One 8X6mm cabo-
chon,
One 8X6mm sterling
silver bezel cup
8 inches of 20-gauge
square wire
14 inches of 14-gauge
half-round wire
5-minute epoxy
Staybrite low tempera-
ture silver solder
Flux

Note
Although
"5-minute epoxy"
cures in five min-
utes, a little longer
time ensures a
permanent bond.

4 Smooth out any bumps or sharp edges of solder under the bezel cup with the Swiss files.

5 Bond the stone into the bezel cup with the 5-minute epoxy. Allow the epoxy to cure for one or two hours (see fig. 3).

FIG. 3

6 Cut one 12- to 14-inch piece of the 14-gauge half-round wire and form a hook on one end (see fig. 4).

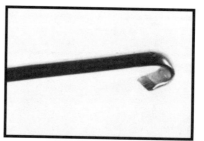

FIG. 4

7 Check your work against pattern 2.

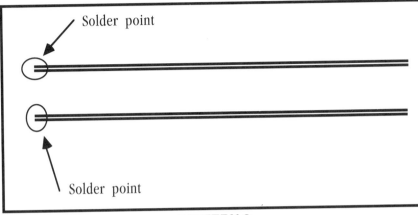

Solder point

Solder point

PATTERN 2

8 Remove the temporary binding wire from the cabochon end of the bundle. Place the hook over the wire bundle as close to the bezel cup as possible. Be certain that the short end of the hook is on the soldered side of the bezel cup. Wrap the bundle for a total of 2 3/16 inch. This will produce a size 6 ring. By adding or subtracting wraps 3/32 inch (between 1/16 and 2/16 inch) you can enlarge or reduce the ring by one size (see fig. 5).

FIG. 5

9 Check your work against pattern 3.

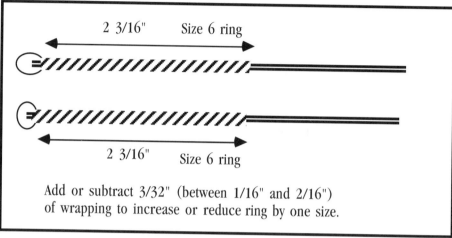

2 3/16"   Size 6 ring

2 3/16"   Size 6 ring

Add or subtract 3/32" (between 1/16" and 2/16")
of wrapping to increase or reduce ring by one size.

PATTERN 3

10 Be sure that the last wrap of the half-round wire is on the same side
of the bundle as the soldered side of the bezel cup. Cut off the remaining half-round wire and file the end to remove sharp edges and
burrs (see fig. 6).

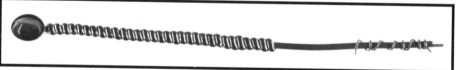

FIG. 6

11 Remove the temporary binding wire from the end of the bundle. Fan out
the two wires and twist each clockwise with the pin vise (see fig. 7).

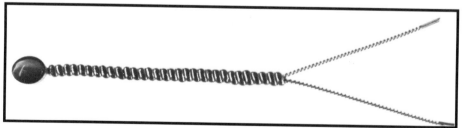

FIG. 7

12 Cut the wires to length using the dimensions on pattern 4.

9/16"

PATTERN 4

13 With the round nose pliers, scroll the two twisted wires (see fig. 8).

FIG. 8

14 Form the ring around the ring mandrel one size smaller than the finished size. Slide the ring up the mandrel to the finished size while holding the ends tightly together (see fig. 9).

FIG. 9

15 Polish the ring while it is still on the mandrel. Make any size or shape adjustments, and the ring is ready to wear.

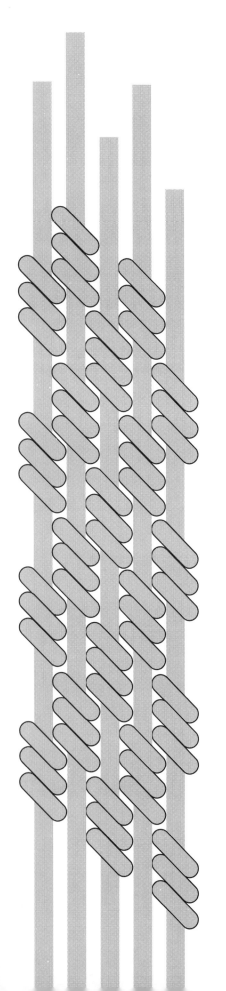

PROJECT 11

Three Solderless Link Chains

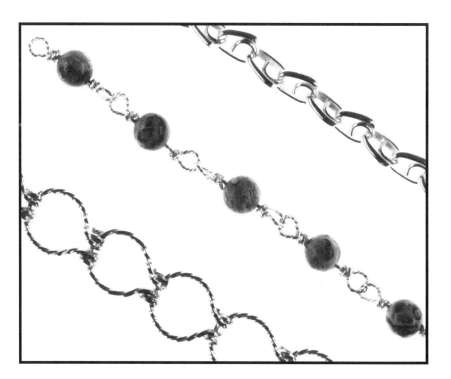

Handformed solderless chains are perfect to accent a wire-wrapped pendant or to wear in conjunction with a wire-wrapped pin or ring. Unfortunately, the repetitious work involved in making these chains is time-consuming and tedious. But give it a chance—you really should try one or two before you decide to buy a commercial chain. Although there are many adequate chains available, nothing sets off a wire-wrapped project like a handcrafted chain. In fact, if you want to exhibit your work, you will find that a handmade chain is an absolute must. In competitions, it could mean a blue ribbon's difference to the judges.

Style A

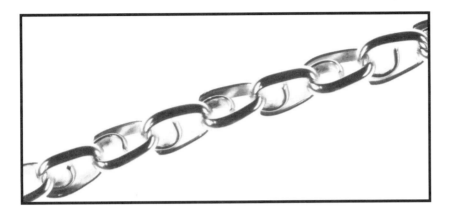

TOOLS REQUIRED:
Pliers
Swiss files set
Polishing cloth

MATERIALS REQUIRED:
14-gauge half-round
 wire.
Clasp

Note
Each link requires
15/16 inch of wire:
5 links equal one
inch of chain.

This "snail link" style is probably the easiest of the three chains to make. The 14-gauge wire is good for bracelets and necklaces. For a finer chain, use 16- or 18-gauge wire and form the links closer to the tip of the round nose pliers.

1 Form a loop on the end of your coil of half-round wire with the round nose pliers. DO NOT PRECUT THE INDIVIDUAL LINKS TO LENGTH. If you have not marked scroll sizes on the jaws of your pliers as described in the techniques section on scrolling, it would be wise to do so now. It is very important to make all the links uniform (see fig. 1).

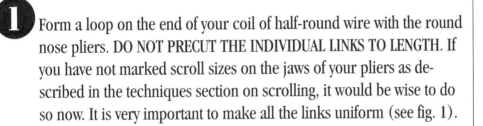

FIG 1

2 Check your work against pattern 1.

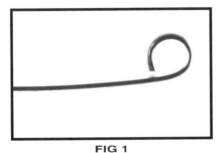

PATTERN 1

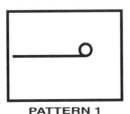

3 Continue forming the wire around the opposite plier jaw until the wire starts to cross the loop (see fig. 2).

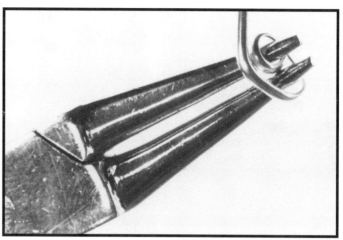

FIG. 2

4 Check your work against pattern 2.

PATTERN 2

5 When the link is fully formed, cut it from the coil at a slight angle across the wire and file the cut end smooth (see pattern 3).

Cut line

PATTERN 3

6 Repeat steps one through three but insert the open part of the second link through the closed part of the first link and close the second link. Continue the process until you have the desired length of chain (see fig. 3).

FIG. 3

7 Double check each link for sharp edges and smooth with a Swiss file. Attach the clasp and polish the chain with the jeweler's cloth. The chain is complete.

TOOLS REQUIRED:
Pin vise
Pliers
Swiss files set
Polishing cloth

MATERIALS REQUIRED:
22-gauge square wire
(2 inches of wire
per link)
One 6mm round full-
drilled bead per link
Clasp

Note

Each link makes
1 1/2 inches of
chain.

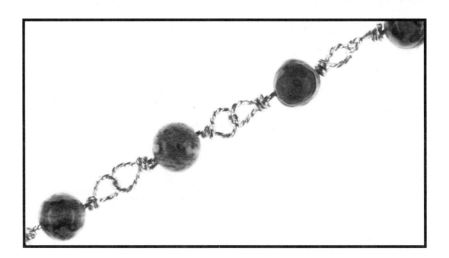

Style B

This style is called the bead link and is a fairly easy link to make. As with the snail link, it is perfect for a necklace or bracelet. The bead link is also very effective when used with a pendant if the pendant's cabochon and the beads are made of the same material.

1 Decide how many links you will require for your chain and twist an appropriate length of the 22-gauge wire using the pin vise and the flat nose pliers. Cut the twisted wire into 2-inch lengths. Take one of the 2-inch pieces of twisted wire and grip it with the round nose pliers 13/16 inch from the end. Form a loop so that the tail of the wire is at 90 degrees to the opposite piece (see fig. 1).

FIG. 1

2 Check your work against pattern 1.

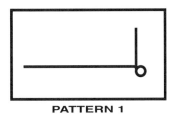

PATTERN 1

3 Wrap the shorter end of wire around the longer end two times. Slide a 6mm bead on the wire, grip the wire 13/16 inch from the end and repeat the wrapping on the opposite end. Clip off the excess wire on the wraps (see fig. 2).

FIG. 2

4 Check your work against pattern 2.

PATTERN 2

5 Start the second link by forming the loop and making the first two wraps. Slide on a 6mm bead, grip the wire 13/16 inch from the end and start forming the loop. Before completing the loop, run the wire end through one of the loops on the first link. Finish forming the loop, make the second two wraps and cut off the excess wire. Repeat the process until you have your desired length of chain (see fig. 3).

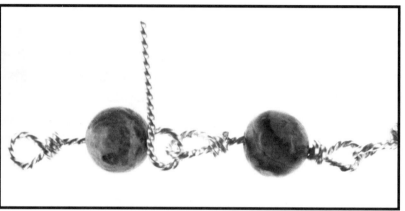

FIG. 3

6 File the cut ends and give the project a good polishing with the jeweler's cloth. Add a clasp and the project is complete.

Style C

TOOLS REQUIRED:
Pin vise
Pliers
Swiss files set
Polishing cloth
Dowel rod or similar
    round shaft approxi-
    mately 5/16 inch in
    diameter.

MATERIALS REQUIRED:
20-gauge square wire
Clasp

Note
    Each link requires
    2 inches of wire.
    Four links make
    1 1/2 inches of
    chain.

This link is the horseshoe and is the most traditional of all wire wrap chains. If the design is too well-known for you, try making the links with 22-gauge wire and placing some small beads on the links before the final forming.

1 Determine the length of wire you will need by multiplying the number of links by 2 inches. Twist the wire with the pin vise and the flat nose pliers until the end in the vise breaks off. Cut the wire into 2-inch pieces and file the ends smooth with a Swiss file.

2 Form the wire evenly around the dowel rod. Put a slight bend on each wire end (see fig. 1).

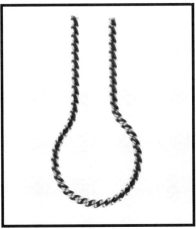

FIG. 1

3 Check your work against pattern 1.

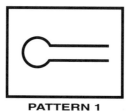

PATTERN 1

4 When you have completed the desired number of links, take one link and scroll the ends back toward the horseshoe end with the round nose pliers. Remember to scroll only one link at this time (see fig. 2).

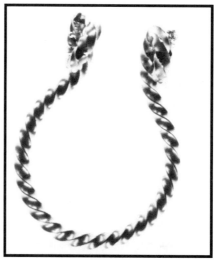

FIG. 2

5 Check your work against pattern 2.

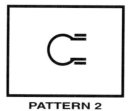

PATTERN 2

6 Take one more link and thread the end through the scrolled loops in the first link. With the round nose pliers, scroll the loops on the second link as you did on the first (see fig. 3).

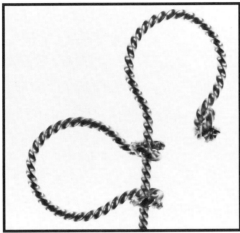

FIG. 3

7 Check your work against pattern 3.

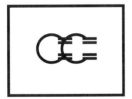

PATTERN 3

8 When you have assembled the desired number of links, bend a loop in the center of a short piece of twisted square wire and place one leg through one of the scrolls on the last link in the chain (see fig. 4).

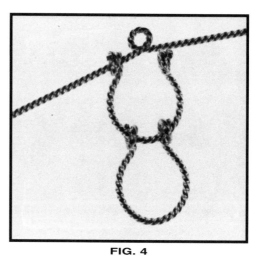

FIG. 4

9 Spread the last link enough to allow you to put the other leg through the opposite scroll. Bend the link back into shape and bend a small scroll on each end of the short wire (see fig. 5).

FIG. 5

Attach the clasp to the loop in the short wire and polish the chain with the jeweler's cloth. The project is complete.

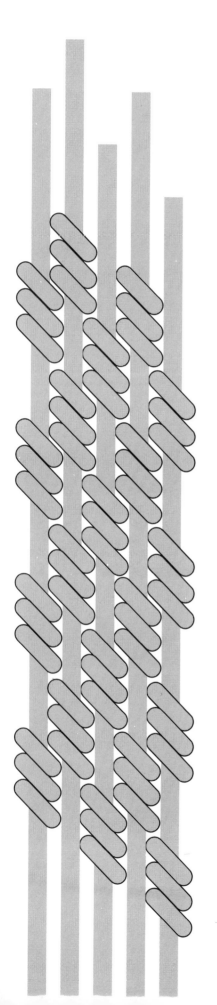

DESIGNING FROM SCRATCH

How to Develop Your Own Projects

We hope the projects that you have completed so far have been challenging and interesting and that you have mastered the basic techniques of wire wrapping. The real fun, however, is designing and wrapping your own creations. This is not as difficult as it sounds; this section will help you take the next step in the craft of wire wrapping.

Up to this point, the stones used have been in calibrated, or standard, sizes. This was done primarily to allow the use of standard dimensions and to use full size patterns in your initial steps. One of the real advantages of wire wrapping, however, is that it is possible to use any size or shape of stone. Silversmithing and lost wax casting provide this advantage, too, but with the disadvantage of the necessity of expensive and space consuming tools. As you have discovered, wire wrapping requires few tools and little space. Follow along now and become a designer as well as a wrapper.

1 The first step in designing a project is to select the stone to be mounted. Standard cabochons, tumbled stones, and faceted stones all make wonderful projects. Sometimes a rough stone with no finishing looks great when wrapped. Very nice, also, are freeform faceted stones sometimes nicknamed "facetchons." Other popular choices are the large crystals of quartz or amethyst-tinged quartz. Coins and medallions are also popular. In short, if you like it, it will be beautiful.

2 Decide whether you want the stone to be caged as in the earrings in projects 2 and 6, or held in prongs as in project 1. In general, if the stone has a flat back, it will look better with a prong-type mount. If it is rounded, it will probably look better in a cage mount. Faceted stones usually look better in prong mounts.

3 Orient the stone so that it will be presented properly. If it is a pendant, it will need to hang with the largest part pointing down. If it is a pin, it might be oriented to the left or to the right. Your eye is usually the best guide, but sketch 1 will show the best orientation for a pendant.

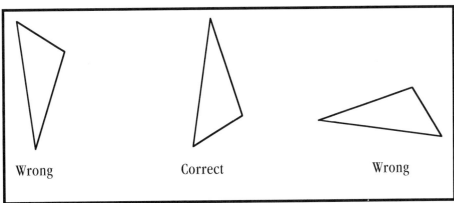

SKETCH 1

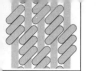

4 After you are satisfied with the orientation of the stone, decide where to put the wires, where to put the wraps, and where to put the scrolls. The simplest way to get started is to use some of your temporary binding or beading wire to make mockups of the piece. From this point, we will be showing the procedure for a prong-type mount. The measuring procedure is the same for a cage-type mount. If you have any difficulties, just review projects 2 and 6.

5 Measure down about 1 inch on a piece of the beading wire, and start forming the wire around the edge of your stone. Continue around to the starting point, bend the wire upward at approximately 90 degrees, and cut the wire off 1 inch above the top of the stone (see sketch 2).

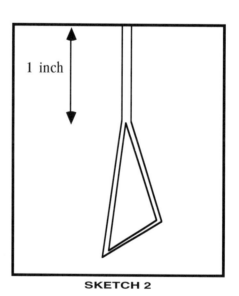

1 inch

SKETCH 2

6 Keep in mind the type of prongs you will be using, and then decide how many wraps you want and where they will be placed (see sketch 3).

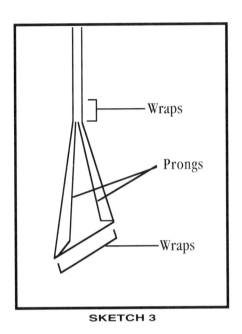

SKETCH 3

7 After deciding the number and location of the wraps, mark the locations on your beading wire. This can be done with an indelible pencil, a permanent marker, or by simply nicking the wire with your steel scale.

8 After the beading wire mockup is complete, choose the type of wire, the gauge, and the cross section. You must also decide how you want to stack the various wires in your bundle (see sketch 4).

Typical wire stacking combinations side views

Back to front wire bundle layouts.

Legend: □T Twisted square wire

□ Square wire

⌒ Half round wire

1. □ T T   3. □ □ T T

2. □ ⌒ T   4. □ ⌒ T T

SKETCH 4

9 When you have chosen your wires, cut them to the same length as the beading wire and bind the ends into a bundle with temporary binding wire.

10 Using an indelible pencil or a permanent marker, transfer the locations of the wrappings from the beading wire to the wire bundle.

11 If you planned to have any of the bundle wires twisted, decide whether they will be twisted before or after the wrappings are applied.

12 If you want your wrappings twisted, twist an appropriate length now. To determine how long a piece you will need, make a full wrap in a scrap wire, unwind it and measure it. Multiply the result by the number of wraps you have decided upon and add an inch or so. Form a hook and wrap the bundle at the locations you marked.

13 Form the bundle around the stone and bind the ends with the temporary binding wire. Form another hook in your wrapping wire and make the wrap on the neck as close to the bend as possible.

14 Form the back prongs with the flat nose pliers and put the stone in position. Form the front prongs and lock the stone in place.

15 To determine the length of the scrolled wires, take a piece of scrap wire and scroll it with the round nose pliers to the size you like. Unroll the scroll and measure the length. Transfer this length to the top wires on your piece and cut them individually. Scroll the wires and the bail loop, give the whole piece a good polishing with the jeweler's cloth, and your project is finished. When first attempting to design a wire wrap project it is sometimes difficult to keep in mind the various parts of the planning. To help you with this stage, we have included a Project Planning Form. On the following page is a sample of the completed form. On the next page is a blank form that you may copy and use in planning your first projects. Keep notes and let your creativity thrive.

1. PROJECT CONFIGURATION: Pendant

2. STONE MATERIAL AND SHAPE: Opal geometric freeform

3. WIRE TYPE (BUNDLE):

1ST	2ND
AWG: 20	AWG:
TYPE: Square	TYPE:
METAL: Gold-filled	METAL:
QTY.: 4 pieces	QTY.:

4. WIRE TYPE (WRAPPINGS):

1ST	2ND
AWG: 12	AWG:
TYPE: Half-round	TYPE:
METAL: Gold-filled	METAL:
QTY.: 2 places	QTY.:

5. BUNDLE STACKING ORDER (BACK TO FRONT):

☐ ☐ T T

6. ESTIMATED WIRE REQUIREMENTS:
    20 inches of 20 AWG. square wire and 4 inches of 12 AWG. half-round wire

7. QUANTITY OF PRONGS:
    4 places—two front side and two backside

8. OTHER FINDINGS REQUIRED: 18-inch spool loom chain

9. SPECIAL NOTES: _____
    _____
    _____

10. CONCEPT SKETCH:

1. PROJECT CONFIGURATION:

2. STONE MATERIAL AND SHAPE:

3. WIRE TYPE (BUNDLE):
   1ST   2ND
     AWG: AWG:
     TYPE: TYPE:
     METAL: METAL:
     QTY.:   QTY.:

4. WIRE TYPE (WRAPPINGS):
   1ST   2ND
     AWG: AWG:
     TYPE: TYPE:
     METAL: METAL:
     QTY.:   QTY.:

5. BUNDLE STACKING ORDER (BACK TO FRONT):

6. ESTIMATED WIRE REQUIREMENTS:

7. QUANTITY OF PRONGS:

8. OTHER FINDINGS REQUIRED:

9. SPECIAL NOTES: _____

   _____

_____

10. CONCEPT SKETCH:

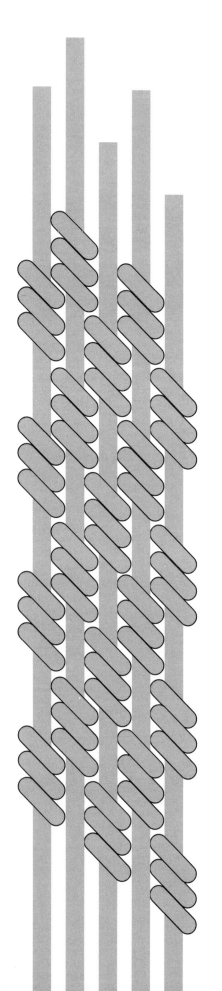

PROJECT 12

A Pair of Freeform Pendants

These two projects will help you start designing your own wire wrapped jewelry. Pendant A uses prong mounting, while B is a simple cage mounting. The type of stone is up to you, and the material requirements will be determined by the size and shape of the stone. You probably won't have a freehand faceted piece of tourmaline in quartz like the one in pendant A, and you may not have a suitable piece of pyrite in white quartz like the one in pendant B. Good choices, however, are a nice tumbled stone with a slightly flattened back for the prong mount, and a choice marble for the cage. Remember, this is the real fun in wire wrapping, so find a stone and enjoy yourself.

Pendant A

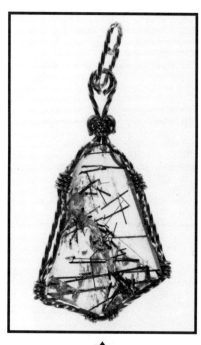

1 Form a piece of temporary binding wire around the circumference of your stone. Leave approximately one inch of extra wire at each end. When the wire is shaped as accurately as possible, decide where you want the wraps and mark the positions on the binding wire (see fig. 1).

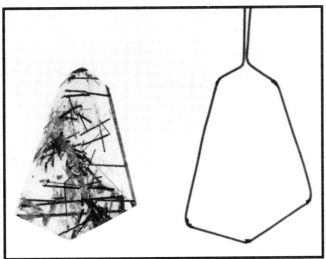

FIG. 1

2 Straighten out the temporary binding wire and measure the length. Cut three pieces of the 20-gauge square wire to the length of the binding wire form. Be sure to leave enough at the ends for the bail loop and any scrolling you may want to do. Form a bundle with the three wires and bind the ends with temporary binding wire. Lay the bundle next to the binding wire form and transfer the wrapping points to the bundle (see fig. 2).

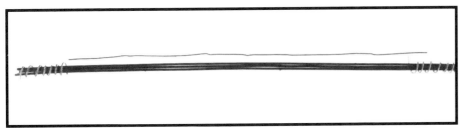

FIG. 2

TOOLS REQUIRED:
Pliers
Pin vise
Swiss files set
Polishing cloth

MATERIALS REQUIRED:
20-gauge square
    wire*
24-gauge square
    wire**
Freeform stone
Temporary binding
    wire

*Length of wire will
    depend upon the
    size of the stone

**24-gauge wire is
    used for the wrap-
    pings to reduce the
    size and give the
    pendant a lighter
    look.

3 Determine the length of wire required for the wraps by using a piece of temporary binding wire as explained in the preceding chapter. Measure a piece of 24-gauge square wire and cut it to the determined length. Place one end in the pin vise and hold the other end with the flat nose pliers. Twist until the end in the pin vise breaks off (see fig. 3).

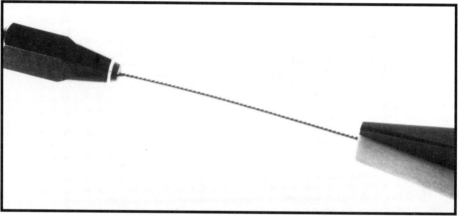

FIG. 3

4 Form one end of the twisted wire into a hook (see fig.4).

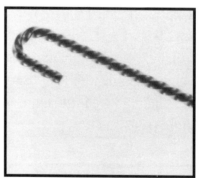

FIG. 4

5 Place the short end of the hook on the bottom of the bundle approximately the thickness of one wire to the right of the center mark. Hold the hook with the flat nose pliers and wrap four wraps to the right. Cut the wire off at the bottom of the bundle. Form another hook and repeat the process on the left side of the center mark. File the cut ends smooth (see fig. 5).

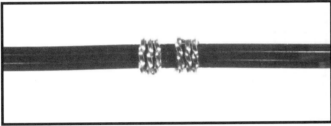

FIG. 5

6 Remove the temporary binding wire from the ends of the bundle and fan the wires out. With the pin vise, twist the front and middle right wires about 10 turns clockwise. Repeat the process on the left side, but be sure to twist counterclockwise (see fig. 6).

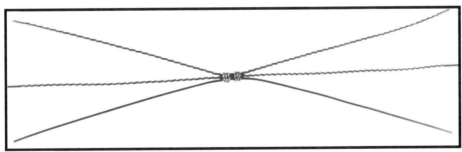

FIG. 6

7 Hold the stone in place on the bottom wraps, and rotate it to verify the position of the intermediate and top sets of wraps. (Since the square wire is thicker than the binding wire used for the form, and the wraps hold it away from the stone slightly, the position of the intermediate and top wraps may have to be adjusted.) Form another hook in the twisted wire and make the left and right intermediate and top wraps. File the ends smooth with a Swiss file (see fig. 7).

FIG. 7

8 Carefully form the bundle around your stone. Allow the bundle ends to cross, then bend them upward and tie them off with temporary binding wire (see fig. 8).

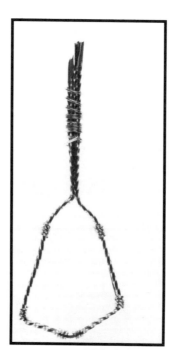 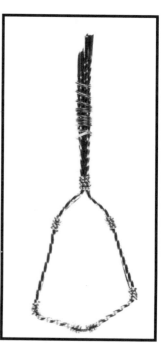

FIG. 8 (LEFT) AND FIG. 9 (RIGHT)

9 Form another hook in the twisted wire, place it as close as possible to the top bends and make four wraps upward. File the cut ends with a Swiss file to remove all sharp edges (see fig. 9).

Grip the rear square wires with the flat nose pliers next to the wrappings and form the back prongs (see fig. 10).

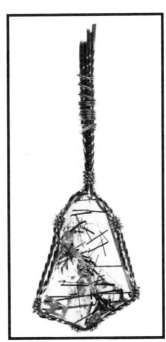

FIG. 10 (LEFT) AND FIG. 11 (RIGHT)

 Insert the stone and make certain that it rests squarely on the back prongs. Using the flat nose pliers, form the front prongs by gripping the front wires next to the wrappings (see fig. 11).

 Remove the temporary binding wire, fan out the top wires and twist the two remaining untwisted wires. Twist just enough to match the other wires (see fig. 12).

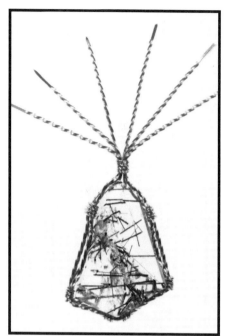

FIG. 12 (RIGHT) AND FIG. 13 (LEFT)

13 Cut the back two wires to the length determined using the method in the preceding chapter. File the sharp edges smooth with the Swiss file and scroll them toward each other to make the bail loop and add the bail. If you wish to have scrolls, follow the same procedure and form the scrolls with the round nose pliers. If you wish to terminate the wires at the end of the neck wrap as shown in fig. 13, cut them to length, file the ends smooth and bend them down with the flat nose or chain nose pliers.

14 Polish the piece with the jeweler's cloth and the project is complete.

Pendant B

TOOLS REQUIRED:
Pin vise
Pliers
Swiss files set
Polishing cloth

MATERIALS REQUIRED:
20-gauge square
   wire*
24-gauge square
   wire**
Stone suitable for a
   cage mount
Temporary binding
   wire

*The amount of wire
   depends on the size
   and shape of the
   stone.

**24-gauge wire is
   used to keep the
   wrappings slightly
   smaller for a lighter
   look.

1 Form a piece of the temporary binding wire around the stone in the approximate shape of the cage. Leave about an inch of extra wire at each end for the dangle loop and the scrolls (see fig. 1).

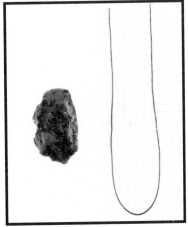

FIG. 1

2 Straighten out the binding wire, measure the length, and cut two pieces of the 20-gauge square wire to that length. Form a bundle and bind each end with temporary binding wire. Mark the center line of the bundle (see fig. 2).

FIG. 2

3 Determine the length of the twisted 24-gauge wrapping wire and cut to length. Place one end in the pin vise and hold the other end with the flat nose pliers. Twist until the end in the pin vise breaks off (see fig. 3).

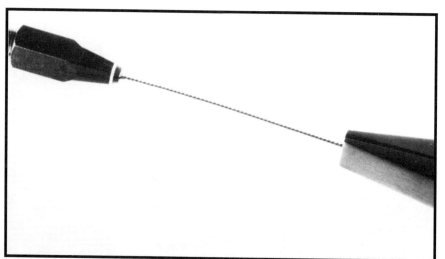

FIG. 3

4 Form a hook in the twisted wire, place it to the right of the center mark on the bundle, and wrap three turns. Cut the wire off on the same side as the short end of the hook. Form another hook and repeat the process on the left side of the bundle. File the cut ends smooth with a Swiss file (see fig. 4).

FIG. 4

5 Remove the temporary binding wire from the ends of the bundle and fan out the wires. Twist the right wires about 10 turns clockwise and the left wires the same number of turns counterclockwise (see fig. 5).

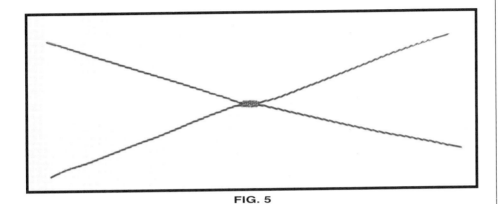

FIG. 5

6 Spread the wires out at 90 degrees to each other (like a large plus sign) and form them around your stone. Gather the wires together at the top and bind them with the temporary binding wire (see fig. 6).

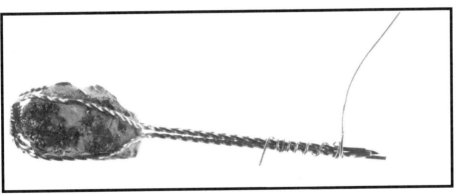

FIG. 6

7 Form a hook in the twisted wrapping wire. Place it as close to the neck bend as possible and wrap four turns upward (see fig. 7).

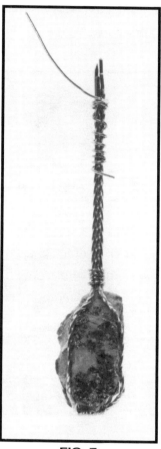

FIG. 7

8 Remove the temporary binding wire and fan the wires out. Determine the length of the bail loop wires and cut them to that length.
File the ends smooth and scroll the wires toward each other. Over-
lap them and form the bail loop. Determine the length of the scroll
wires and cut them to that length. Form the scrolls with the round
nose pliers (see fig. 8).

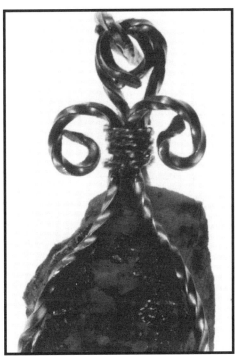

FIG. 8

9 Adjust the cage wires until you are pleased with their position and
shape. Adjust the scrolls if necessary. Attach a bail, give the project a
final polishing with the jeweler's cloth and the project is finished.

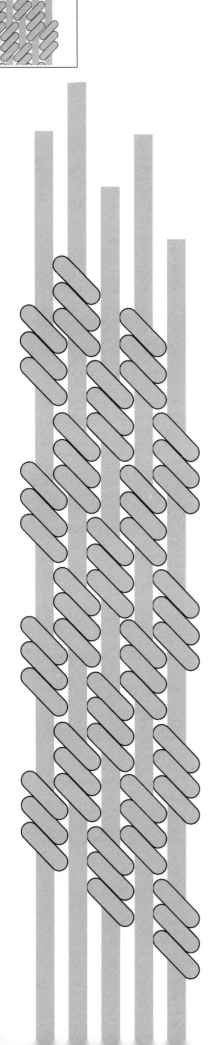

Sources

The tools and materials needed for wire wrapping are available at rock shops, lapidary supply stores, and some larger crafts stores.

The following three magazines carry advertisements from a great number of suppliers, and often carry articles on wire wrapping. They also publish annual buyer's guides that list suppliers throughout the United States.

ROCK AND GEM MAGAZINE
4880 Market Street
Ventura, CA 93003

JEWELRY CRAFTS
4880 Market Street
Ventura, CA 93003

LAPIDARY JOURNAL
Devon Office Center, Suite 201
60 Chestnut Avenue
Devon, PA 19333

The following Gem Guides publication is also available for additional information and designs.

HOW TO MAKE WIRE JEWELRY, Jenkins and Thrasher. Step-by-step instructions and color illustrations show how to use inexpensive tools and supplies to make pins, pendants, chains, rings, bracelets, earrings, stickpins and novelties. 32 pages, $5.00.

Wire Gauge Chart

This chart will help you choose the gauge and shape of wire used for wire wrap projects.

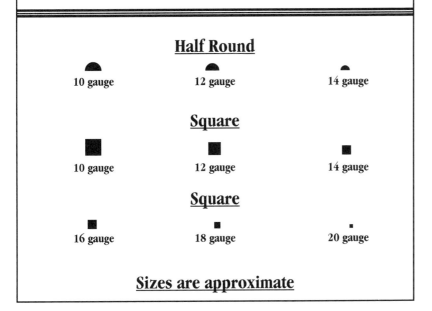

Half Round

10 gauge   12 gauge   14 gauge

Square

10 gauge   12 gauge   14 gauge

Square

16 gauge   18 gauge   20 gauge

Sizes are approximate

About The Authors

Curtis Leonard's interest in jewelry making began nearly 16 years ago, when he was about 15. His stepfather brought packets of jewelry and gemstones from his frequent trips to the Orient, and Curtis' interest was caught. Just admiring the stones and jewelry were soon not enough for young Curtis, however, so he began to learn the skills of wireworking, stone cutting and polishing, silversmithing and goldsmithing, and stone setting.

After earning a degree in liberal arts from Orange Coast College in Costa Mesa, California, and a Bachelor of Science degree in business administration at the University of Redlands, California, he founded Curtis Kenneth Leonard Enterprises, which specializes in importing, cutting, and setting gemstones. Despite his business demands, Curtis still finds time to devote to one of his first loves—wire wrapping. He has demonstrated his techniques and craftsmanship to many individuals and groups, and his work has been exhibited at numerous gem and mineral shows and county fairs. Most recently, his work was awarded a first place blue ribbon at the Orange County, California, fair.

William Kappele's interest in jewelry making and rockhounding began nearly 30 years ago during camping trips with his wife, Cora, and sons, Bill and Richard. As his collection began to overrun the garage and backyard, William took up lapidary in self defense. For the past eight years he has written for *Rock and Gem Magazine* and is currently a contributing editor. William contributed his editing and photography expertise to this book and, although fascinated by wire wrapping he had seen at gem shows, he was a novice when this book began. Watching Curtis and working with the text and photos has infected him with the wire wrap virus, however, and he may never be the same.